A WILLIAMSON ★ KIDS CAN! BOOK

KIDS LEARN AMERICA!

BRINGING GEOGRAPHY TO LIFE WITH PEOPLE, PLACES & HISTORY

PATRICIA GORDON & REED C. SNOW

DESIGN & ILLUSTRATION
• TREZZO BRAREN STUDIO •

WILLIAMSON PUBLISHING CO. CHARLOTTE, VERMONT 05445

Copyright © 1992 by Patricia Gordon and Reed C. Snow

Library of Congress
Cataloging-in-Publication Data

Gordon, Patricia, 1938–
    Kids learn America! : bringing geography to life with
people, places, and history / Patricia Gordon and
Reed C. Snow; illustrations by Loretta Trezzo
        p.   cm.
    Includes bibliographical references and index.
    Summary: Surveys the geography, history, and culture
of the states and territories of the United States.
    ISBN 0-913589-58-6
    1. United States—Geography—Juvenile literature. 2.
United States —Civilization—Juvenile literature. (1.
United States.)
    I. Snow, Reed C., 1934-   . II. Trezzo, Loretta, ill. III. Title.
E161.3.G67   1991   91-27245
973—dc20   CIP
                                                  AC
Cover and page design: Trezzo-Braren Studio
Illustrations: Loretta Trezzo
Printing: Capital City Press

Williamson Publishing Co.
Box 185
Charlotte, Vermont 05445
(800) 234-8791

Manufactured in the United States of America

10

Selected illustrations taken from the following books:

American Indian Design and Decoration
by Le Roy H. Appleton (Dover Publications, Inc., 1971)
Animals
Selected by Jim Harter (Dover Publications, Inc. 1979)
Art Archives
Harry Bigelow Coffin, Editor (Art Archives Press, 1950)
The Century Illustrated Monthly Magazine
Volumes I through LXXVII (The Century Company, 1891)
Cuts, Borders, and Ornaments
Selected from the Robinson-Pforzheimer Typographical Collection (The New York Public Library, 1962)
Decorative Art of the Southwestern Indians
Dorothy Smith Sides (Dover Publications, Inc. 1985)
Dover Clip Art Series:
        Animal Silhouettes
        Designed by Ellen Sandbeck (Dover Publications, Inc. 1989)
        Illustrations for Holidays and Special Occasions
        Designed by Ed Sibbert, Jr. (Ed Sibbert Jr., 1983)
        Old Fashioned Animal Cuts
        Designed by Carol Belanger Grafton (Dover Publications, Inc. 1987)
        Old Fashioned Patriotic Cuts
        Designed by Carol Belanger Grafton (Dover Publications, Inc. 1988)
        Old Fashioned Sports Illustrations
        Designed by Carol Belanger Grafton (Dover Publications, Inc. 1988)
        Graphic Products Corporation (1986 through 1989
Early Floral Engravings
Emanuel Sweerts (Dover Publications, Inc. 1976)
Pictorial History of the United States: Vol. I & Vol. 2
Henry Davenport Northrop (J.R. Jones, 1901)
Graphic Source Clip Art Book Library:
        Classic Comic Cuts
        Floral Ornaments
        Food Art
        Graphic Symbols
        Printers Ornaments
        Printers Silhouettes
        Super Shapes
        Sports
        Sport Silhouettes
Graphic Products Corporation (1986 through 1989
Handbook of Early American Advertising Art
by Clarence P. Hornung (Dover Publications, Inc. 1956)
Hands
Selected by Jim Hauter (Dover Publications, Inc. 1985)
1890 Woodcuts by Thomas Bewick and His School
edited by Blanche Cirker (Dover Publications, Inc. 1962)
Old Engravings and Illustrations

CONTENTS

A C K N O W L E D G E M E N T S

Thank you LaNae and Jim, and the Gordon and Snow kids.

How fortunate we all are that Susan and Jack Williamson have the vision of what Kids Can Do. Thank you

HELLO AMERICA!

What's a periscope doing spying on New Jersey and the Atlantic Ocean? What do a prehistoric bird, a fat cannon, and a leaping frog have in common? You'll find out! Is it true that part of one state looks like a shark? Welcome to the wonderful world of *Kids Learn America!* It's challenging and exciting, and it's all about that wonderful place — the USA.

There is something to do (and lots to think about) on every page. Just to keep all of you on your toes, we'll see if you can "Catch A Clue," as we give you hints and then challenge you to solve the mini-mysteries in every state. We'll take you to every corner of the country and introduce you to a lot of famous people (and some who should be!). There's no rest for the weary, as you criss-cross the USA.

Munchy, crunchy caramel corn and a scrumptious peach cobbler are yours for the making, and you can do it yourself. Try your hand at planting a container garden New Jersey-style or, if you're in the mood for something southwestern, turn it into a cactus garden. Activities, games, and recipes, too, will help all Kids Learn America!....but mostly there will be a lot of fun as you discover the individual personality of each state and how states are similar in some ways, yet differ in other ways from their neighbors.

Speaking of neighbors, we have divided the country into seven regions to make it a little easier to understand the geography, history, and culture of the USA. Of course, every state is different, but certain large areas share geographical features such as the Rocky Mountain states, and other regions share a part of history, such as the New England and Mid-Atlantic states' involvement in the Revolutionary War. As you'll see, grouping states together makes it a lot easier to know where they are and what they are like.

There's so much to do and so much to "see" — why don't you grab some pencils, paper, crayons, perhaps a friend or brother or sister (or just curl up someplace cozy by yourself), and let's begin to discover America now!

C O L O R   A M E R I C A !

How about lighting up the United States with a rainbow of colors on your Color America! map? Now it's your chance to beautify America with a few strokes of a crayon. The colors suggested in each state's Color America! section will remind you of something about that state. Discover how each state has its own personality and how their differences give this country such a unique flavor.

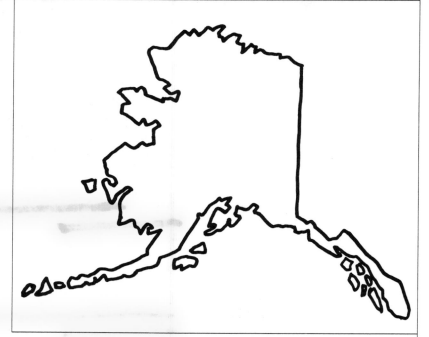

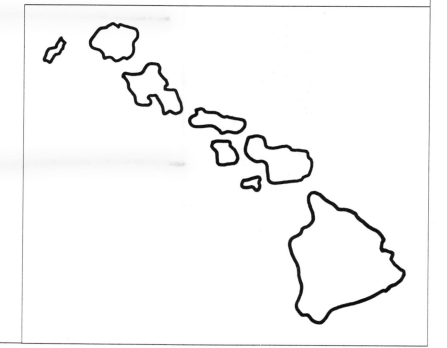

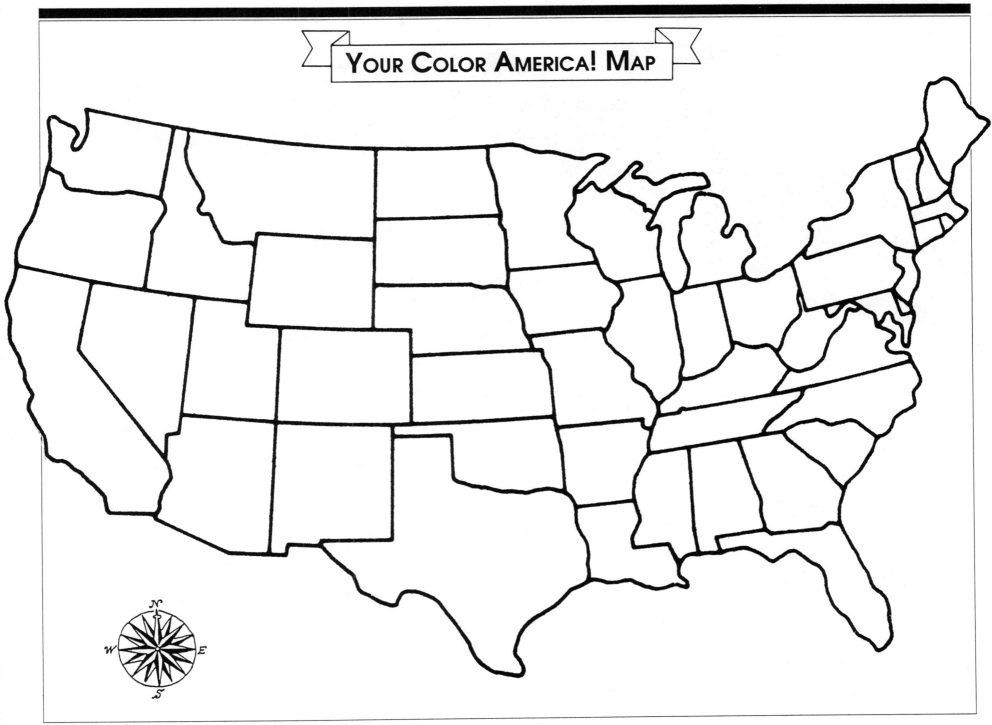

YOUR COLOR AMERICA! MAP

THE NEW ENGLAND STATES

N A M E   T H E   C A P I T A L

How many capitals of the New England states can you name? Write the names below, then check your answers on the state maps. Each state capital is marked with a ✪. Did you get all six state capitals correct?

CONNECTICUT _____

MAINE _____

MASSACHUSETTS _____

NEW HAMPSHIRE _____

RHODE ISLAND _____

VERMONT _____

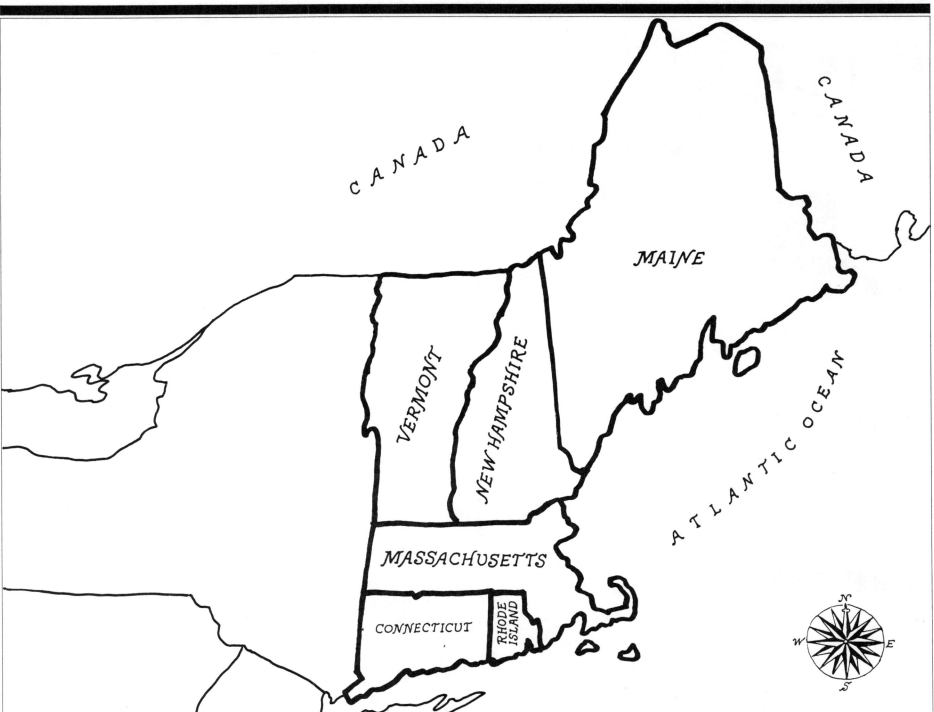

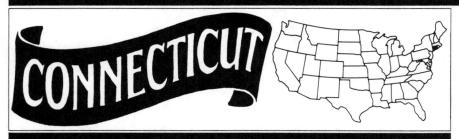

Connecticut's state song says, "Yankee Doodle went to town riding on a pony, stuck a feather in his cap and called it macaroni." What color do you think the feather was? How about coloring Connecticut the feather color that you like best.

"**Y**ankee Doodle," an all-American favorite, is the state song of the *Constitution State* — the first state in the New World to have a written constitution. Named Quinnechtukgut by the Indians — which means "beside the long tidal river" — we now know that "river" as Long Island Sound. This state of great forests, plains, beaches, and bays is home to the world's first atomic submarine, the U.S. Coast Guard Academy, and hockey's Hartford Whalers. Connecticut has Yankee spirit and Yankee pride!

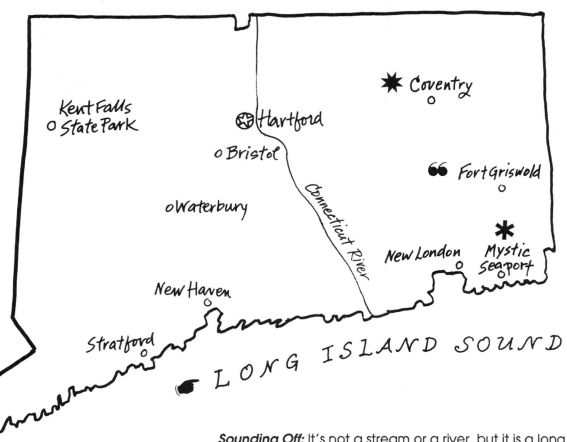

MAPTALK

Sounding Off: It's not a stream or a river, but it is a long passage of water. It is located between large bodies of land or between an island and the mainland. This long, usually narrow passage of water is called a sound. Locate Connecticut and New York. Can you find the Long Island Sound that separates these two states? Now, see if you can find Norton Sound in Alaska, Puget Sound in Washington, and Albemarle and Pamlico sounds in North Carolina. Use an atlas, U.S. map, or a globe.

THE CURIOUS W's

 Who? I was spying behind British lines on Long Island while trying to discover when the Redcoats were planning to attack New York. The British said they would spare my life if I denounced America. I refused, and I was hanged. Who am I?
(answer: Nathan Hale; Coventry)

 What? I am an arm of the Atlantic Ocean between Connecticut and New York. Along my shoreline are coves and tiny bays. People are now working very hard to save the beautiful shorebirds along my banks. Do you know what I am?

(answer: Long Island Sound on the southern boundary of Connecticut)

 Where? Great whaling ships docked here in the early 19th century. Today, the Australia, the oldest American schooner afloat, is here along with New England's last wooden whaling ship. Do you know the name of this Connecticut port city?
(answer: Mystic Seaport, in Mystic)

 Why? When the British stormed Fort Griswold, 150 Americans were no match for 800 Redcoats. And guess what? The British commander had been an American general, but he changed sides! Why is Fort Griswold part of our American history?

(answer: The general was Benedict Arnold who will always be remembered as a traitor to his country.)

LIGHTS, CAMERA, ACTION! Make a movie in your mind. Picture a giant *heart* flopping around in the back of a *Ford* truck. What keeps the heart from bouncing out of the truck? It's connected to a rope! You now know the capital of Connecticut. Heart + Ford = Hartford. Connected = Connecticut. Can you remember Hartford, Connecticut?

 **HIP, HIP, HOORAY!**

Get acquainted with two of America's favorite characters, Tom Sawyer and Huckleberry Finn, created by Samuel Clemens, better known to everyone as Mark Twain. Have you read about their wild adventures? Twain lived and wrote in Connecticut for 30 years, mostly at Nook Farm.

 **CATCH A CLUE**

 Noah Webster was a friend to children and a man of many words. In 1828, he wrote a book that made him very famous. It was a
(a) dictionary
(b) encyclopedia
(c) almanac
(answer: (a); clue: words = dictionary)

CONNECTICUT

PACK YOUR BAGS

People who know rods and reels are in the right place in this sporting state. There is fishing galore in the many Connecticut rivers and out of ports on deep-sea fishing boats. If you really want some high adventure, rumor has it that Captain Kidd, the infamous pirate, buried valuable treasures on one of the Thimble Islands. Now all you have to do is find the right island. There are 365 of them!

WHO SAID THAT?

As he stood on the gallows platform about to be hanged by the British, a great American patriot said, "I only regret that I have but one life to lose for my country." He was Nathan Hale, and he was only 21 years old.

Ⓒ Ⓐ Ⓣ Ⓒ Ⓗ Ⓐ Ⓒ Ⓛ Ⓤ Ⓔ

A 25-inch person named Tom Thumb and Jumbo the Elephant were stars of P.T. Barnum's traveling show. Barnum was one of the greatest showmen in the world. What traveling show did he start in 1871?
(a) Circus Vargas
(b) Picadilly Circus
(c) The Greatest Show on Earth
(answer: (c); clue: greatest showmen = Greatest Show)

PICTURE THIS

Connecticut looks like a rectangle except for the southwest corner. This part of the state looks like a waterspout. Can you imagine the state of Connecticut filled with water that is pouring out of the spout? When you think of Connecticut, think of this waterspout shape at the southwest corner. Do you suppose all of the water could come from the Connecticut River, which is the largest river in the state?

SHOP TALK

Every time you "Pin the Tail on the Donkey" or put a lock on your bicycle, say, "thank you" to these early industrialists of Connecticut: John I. Howe invented a pin-making machine; Linus Yale invented the cylinder lock. By the way, if you're wearing cotton clothes right now, thank Eli Whitney. He invented the cotton gin, which takes the seeds out of cotton!

Just Like... Old

Suddenly the lamps went out and the room was instantly dark. A door opened amid the confusion. When the candles were relighted, someone in the room yelled that the charter had disappeared! (The charter was a document that gave land and certain rights to our colony.) The British wanted it back, because they wanted to change it, but someone had bolted out of the room when the lamps were snuffed and had hidden the charter in the hollow of an old oak tree — known long after as the Charter Oak — to keep it out of the hands of the British. Hurrah!

You can make your own charter. Simply take a piece of white paper, dip it in water mixed with a little cider vinegar, and let it dry. Then write your declaration in your fanciest handwriting or calligraphy, "Hear ye, hear ye! Let it be known to all, the olde land northward from ye river....." To make your charter look even more authentic, ask an adult to help as you hold it over a burning candle, just close enough so spots are scorched but not burned in the paper. You might even lightly burn off a corner of the paper. Now, roll the paper and seal it with some melted wax. It's as good as old!

HOW'S YOUR LATITUDE ATTITUDE?

Are Hartford, Connecticut and Rome, Italy on the same approximate latitude (41°N) as Kansas City, Kansas or Springfield, Missouri?

WHO SAID THAT?

"In the spring I have counted one hundred and thirty-six different kinds of weather inside of twenty-four hours," said Mark Twain, a famous American writer. He was talking about the changeable Connecticut weather. Do you think he was exaggerating?

Honey bees aren't all the same, but we usually think of them as black and yellow. If you color Maine black and yellow stripes on your America! map, it will help you remember the state insect. It's the honey bee.

Sunshine strikes the state of Maine before it shines on any other state in our nation. Why? Because Maine is farther east than all the rest. The *Pine Tree State* has thousands of offshore islands, harbors, and coves for excellent sailing and fishing. Portland Head Light, the oldest lighthouse along Maine's rugged shoreline, dates back to 1791. Cool summers, long, cold winters, fog along the craggy coast, all say, "Hello, Maine!"

You Can Do It!

What rises nearly a mile high in the sky of Maine? And, how many feet are in a mile? To make *Mount Katahdin*, Maine's highest mountain, exactly one mile high (5,280 feet in a mile), a 13-foot tower was erected at its peak. Can you figure out how tall Mount Katahdin is without the tower? Sure, you can.

Getting Ready: The word *sphere* means shaped like a ball. The earth is shaped like a ball, so the earth is a sphere. *Hemi* means half, so *hemisphere* means half of a ball or half of the earth. The earth has two hemispheres—North and South— if you cut it in half one way or it has two other hemispheres—East and West—if you cut it in half the other way. Hemisphere = half a sphere. Great! You're good at this!

Moosehead Lake

Mt. Katahdin

Longfellow Mts.

○ Bangor

Machias

✪ Augusta

✳ Acadia National Park

Brunswick ○

Portland

Portland Head Light

PICTURE THIS

See if you can make out the side view of a man's face looking east at Canada. Part of his chin is touching the Atlantic Ocean. Start at the top. Can you see the long, flat forehead, the little pug nose, his open mouth, and a chin that sticks out? If you can't, try putting your finger at the top of the state and following the boundary down to the Atlantic Ocean. Got it?

THE CURIOUS W's

 Who? I hated slavery and I wrote *Uncle Tom's Cabin*, a book about the American slaves' terrible living conditions and treatment. Some say my book was one of the causes of the Civil War. Who am I?
(answer: Harriet Beecher Stowe, who wrote her book in Brunswick)

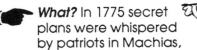 **What?** In 1775 secret plans were whispered by patriots in Machias, Maine, plotting to take over a British ship. Their plan worked, and the ship was captured in the first naval battle of the Revolutionary War. Have you ever heard of the British ship?
(answer: The Margaretta)

Where? Hiking and biking trails wind through the ragged cliffs and tiny coves of *Acadia National Park*. It is the only national park in the northeastern United States. North Atlantic sea birds make their home here and when the snow melts, hundreds of wildflowers bloom. Can you find Acadia National Park? Look southeast of Bangor.

Why? "Listen, my children, and you shall hear of the midnight ride of Paul Revere..." are the opening words of the poem, "Paul Revere's Ride." Who wrote this poem and why is it so famous?
(answer: Henry Wadsworth Longfellow, who was born in Portland, wrote his poem about an important event in the Revolutionary War.)

Make a movie in your mind. Picture a lion with a long, shaggy *mane*. What's happening to the mane? *A gust* of wind is blowing the lion's mane so hard that it's standing straight up from his head. And what's the name of this state? mane = Maine. And the capital? Remember that *a gust of wind is blowing the mane* straight up. A gust = Augusta. Augusta is the capital of Maine. Easy, isn't it?

Rub-a-Dub-Leaves

It's easy to make your own "autumn show" of color. All you'll need are: a brown grocery bag or large piece of paper, scissors, crayons (old broken ones work best), and a collection of leaves of any shape or size. Place leaves one at a time under the paper. If you're using a grocery bag, be sure the printed side is facing down. Using the side of a fall-colored crayon, rub back and forth over the leaf until you can see its imprint. Continue to rub over leaves one at a time, sometimes overlapping, until you have a leaf collage. It will bring you autumn no matter where you live! Give it a try. You can use the same technique on different sized paper to make stationery, cards, wrapping paper, or covers for your school books.

Maine has one honor that no other state can claim:
(a) it is bordered by only one other state.
(b) It grows more apples than any other state.
(c) It grows more cranberries than any other state.
(answer: (a); clue: one honor = one other state)

Over 20 ski resorts open when the flakes start to fall. Dog sled racing, ice fishing, and unusual events like canoeski—paddling a canoe down a giant slalom course instead of using skis—put warm smiles on cold faces. Summertime brings lobster feasts and clambakes along the coast to remind people of Maine's ties to the sea. Something fun is always going on in Maine.

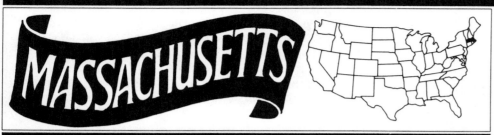

MASSACHUSETTS

COLOR AMERICA!

Do you know the color of the cranberries grown in the bogs of Cape Cod? Deep red might be a good color for Massachusetts on your America! map. Do you know the holiday when the most cranberries are eaten in the United States? Thanksgiving? You're absolutely right!

Survival was what Native Americans such as Massasoit, Samoset, and Squanto gave to the Pilgrims. Massachusetts, meaning "near the great hill," was the Indian name given to the area. Celebrated events, bold patriots, and heroes tie all Americans to Massachusetts' historical beginnings. Walden Pond, Salem, and Tanglewood are meaningful American locations. Cape Cod and the islands, Nantucket and Martha's Vineyard, blend flavors of the past and present. The Bay State is one of our country's historic treasures.

Berkshire Hills

Quabbin Reservoir

Concord

Lexington

Salem

Cambridge

Boston

Old Sturbridge Village

Springfield

Plymouth

Provincetown

Cape Cod Bay

Cape Cod

Hyannis

Martha's Vineyard

Nantucket

MAPTALK

Where on the World Are You?: Put a rubber band around the middle of an orange, going from left to right. The top half is the north, or the Northern Hemisphere, and the bottom half is the south, or the Southern Hemisphere. Turn the orange so that the rubber band goes up and down. Now, on your left is the Western Hemisphere and on your right is the Eastern Hemisphere. Now you know the earth's four hemispheres. Do you know which two hemispheres the United States is in?

THE CURIOUS W's

 Who? "The British are coming!" was the warning call I shouted to the folks of Lexington and the surrounding countryside. I rode a borrowed horse late that night of April 18, in 1775. I was a silversmith by trade, but I'm most famous for my midnight ride. Who am I?
(answer: Paul Revere; Boston)

What? America's first college was founded because some Puritan fathers wanted their sons to get a good education. In fact, one hundred dads got together, and 16 years after the Mayflower landed at Plymouth, a college was started. What is this famous school?
(answer: Harvard University; Cambridge)

Where? Ben Franklin's cow grazed here. Over the years, hangings took place, soldiers practiced drills, and people were buried here. Frog Pond was where persons who broke some laws were dunked as punishment. Today, Swan boats take people for lazy summer day rides. Where is this oldest public park in America?
(answer: Boston Common, in the center of old Boston)

Why? The drum roll sounded and 70 men, young and old, gathered on Lexington's village green. A regiment of Redcoats faced us and we were told to go to our homes. We refused. No one knows who fired the first shot, but this event changed America forever. Why are Lexington and Concord important to our history?
(answer: fighting there started the Revolutionary War)

Make a movie in your mind. Picture the *boss* of a fish store with a huge one-*ton* fish between his teeth. What is he doing? Why, he's chewing that one-ton fish! You've just learned the capital of Massachusetts. Boss + ton = Boston. And the State? Picture the boss *chewing*. Chew = Massachusetts. Boston, Massachusetts. You've got it!

HIP, HIP, HOORAY!

"It's a touchdown!" "He shoots, he scores. . . it's a goal!" "It's a three-run triple!" are words Bay Staters like to hear. They love sports, and who wouldn't with great teams and great players to watch. Larry Bird and the NBA Boston Celtics play in historic Boston Garden. Hockey's Boston Bruins make their home at the Garden, too. Bobby Orr, one of hockey's all-time superstars was a Bruin. The NFL New England Patriots play football in Foxboro. Anyone who collects baseball cards knows the value of Red Sox players Ted Williams, Carl Yastrzemski, and Wade Boggs, but do you know what America's oldest long distance race is? It's the Boston Marathon, and every spring for nearly 100 years, people have run through the streets and over the hills of Boston.

MASSACHUSETTS

WHO SAID THAT?

"Don't fire until you see the whites of their eyes!" is what Colonel William Prescott told the colonists as they dug in to fight the British on Breed's (Bunker) Hill overlooking Boston.

 C A T C H A C L U E

Ready to fight at a minute's notice, these American colonials fought the British until the regular Revolutionary Army was organized. What were these brave patriots called?

(a) Continentals
(b) Minutemen
(c) Burgesses

(answer: (b); clue: minute = Minutemen)

KITCHEN·CULTURE

Fireworks and dragon parades light up Boston's Chinatown in February. The Irish have their day, too. St. Patrick's Day parades and festivities beckon to young and old for the wearin' of the green on March 17th. In the Berkshires, the Scots tune up their bagpipes for the Highland Games in May. All lads and lassies are welcome. And don't forget to treat yourself to authentic Italian food when the Italians of Boston's North End come alive during summer weekends with street fairs honoring Saint's Day. The Portuguese of Fall River and the Greeks of Lowell all add to the ethnic culture which makes Massachusetts a true blend of America. And every festivity has its own special foods!

Get a taste for the whole world right in your own kitchen by eating foods that come from other places. Try to match these foods to their country. It's really as easy as ABC. Just write the right country next to the food.

1.	Hot Dogs	China
2.	Chow Mein	Mexico
3.	Fish and Chips	Italy
4.	Quiche	America
5.	Frankfurter	Ireland
6.	Baklava	Japan
7.	Potatoes	Germany
8.	Spaghetti	England
9.	Sushi	Greece
10.	Taco	France

(answer: Put the countries in alphabetical order, and you have the answers right.)

PACK YOUR BAGS

Massachusetts has more historic sites than there were witches in Salem in 1692! You can even see a costumed reenactment of the Boston Tea Party in Boston Harbor in December, the Minutemen marching to Concord in April, and walk the Freedom Trail in Boston any time of year. Don't miss the Cape Cod National Seashore and the New Bedford Whaling Museum. Speaking of whales, have you ever gone whale watching? Bay Staters can do this for six months starting in October aboard whaling cruise boats that leave from Gloucester or Provincetown. Thar she blows!

Peach Baskets?

Two peach baskets and one soccer ball were all it took. The baskets were attached to a 10' high elevated running track in the Springfield YMCA gym, one basket at each end. When the P.E. director asked the kids to come up with a team game that they could play inside during the cold, winter months, James Naismith, a young assistant, came up with the peach basket idea, and the kids loved it. That was 100 years ago. It would look a little strange to see someone slam-dunking in a peach basket today, but Naismith's game is now called basketball and guess what? The "baskets" are still 10' high! How would you like to invent a brand new game? Think about it.

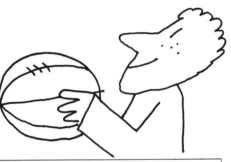

C A T C H A C L U E

The oldest warship afloat in any navy in the world is the USS Constitution in Boston Harbor. It got its nickname during the War of 1812 when someone said that canon shot bounced off its solid oak hull. The Constitution's nickname is
(a) "Old Ironsides"
(b) "Merrimac"
(c) "Constellation"
(answer: (a); clue: oldest = Old)

PICTURE THIS

Look for the hook! It's on the east side of Massachusetts, the state that's shaped like a rectangle until it meets the Atlantic Ocean. What could you catch on this hook in Cape Cod Bay? How about a cod fish? Catching a cod fish on the hook of Massachusetts will help you remember the shape of the state and the state fish. Which is? The cod!

NEW HAMPSHIRE

Robert Frost was a famous poet who spent many years of his life in New Hampshire and Vermont. Have you ever noticed how ice, frost, and snow sometimes look pale blue? Wouldn't this be a good color for New Hampshire on your America! map? It might help you remember Robert Frost and his wonderful poems. Many are about New England's beautiful landscapes.

Majestic alpine vistas in the White Mountains have given New Hampshire one of its nicknames, the Switzerland of America. It is also known as the *Granite State*, because of its vast granite deposits and quarries. New Hampshire was the first colony to declare its freedom from British rule, and today, the English influence is still seen in New Hampshire's little hamlets, villages, and cities. From its 18-mile Atlantic coastline to its Indian-named rivers and lakes, New Hampshire is a forested wonderland of nature.

WHO SAID THAT?

"Go West, young man" is the advice he gave to all of the young men in New York who couldn't find a job. He borrowed the words from someone else, but Horace Greely, from Amherst, New Hampshire, is the person who gets the credit.

Mount Washington

Franconia Notch

White Mountains

Hanover

Franklin

Concord ⊛

Portsmouth

Manchester

MAPTALK

Latitude Ladders: Grab an orange (or draw one), and put an elastic around its middle, so that it's equal distance from the top to the bottom. Call this rubber band the *equator.* Now, pretend that you are teensy-tiny and that you want to hike up the side of the orange to the tippy top (the North Pole). Being a clever sort, you put more elastic bands around the orange, spacing them evenly in a ladder-like fashion. Now you can climb to the North Pole by walking on your ladder of imaginary *latitude* lines which circle the earth. These lines are equal distances apart, just like the steps of a real ladder. Ladder= latitude. Whew! You made it. Take a rest and then head for the South Pole.

THE CURIOUS W's

Who? My father was a New Hampshire judge, but I landed in politics. I ended up being a great speaker, and I loved the United States. I was secretary of state for three presidents. Who am I? Hint: I'm not the one who wrote the dictionary.
(answer: Daniel Webster; in Franklin)

What? Two surveyors, washing themselves in Profile Lake, looked up and were amazed at what they saw. It was the perfect profile of a man's face carved out of the stony mountain by the wind and weather. What is the name of this natural wonder?
(answer: The Old Man of the Mountain; Franconia Notch)

Where? If you had been standing on top of Mount Washington on April 12, 1934, you might have been blown off! This was the day the world record was set for the highest recorded wind ever. Can you imagine the wind blowing a treacherous 231 miles per hour? It did! Where is Mount Washington?
(answer: White Mountains)

Why? Dartmouth College began as a college for Native American Indians and other youths. Samson Occom, an Indian, raised enough money to start the college in Hanover. Why are the Native Americans of the Six Nations Confederation happy about what Occom did?
(answer: Their tuition today at Dartmouth is free.)

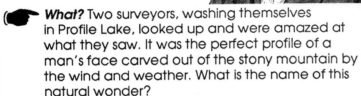

Make a movie in your mind. Picture the *Concord* jet landing in your backyard. How could this happen? Because the pilot and co-pilot of the plane are two *hamsters*, wearing sun glasses! Concord jet = Concord. Hamsters = New Hampshire. Concord is the capital of New Hampshire, and now you know another state and its capital. You're doing great!

Chilling, Isn't It?

A cooling wind feels great when the temperature is hot, but wind can be dangerous if the apparent temperature drops due to the windchill factor. When the wind blows and the temperature is cold, you will have to bundle up even more to protect yourself. The National Weather Service has devised a chart to help determine windchill. Find the temperature across the top line and the speed of the wind on the far left-hand column. Read the temperature on the spot where the lines meet to find out how the windchill factor makes it colder than the thermometer says.

• TEMPERATURE •

		35°	30°	25°	20°	15°	10°	5°	0°	5°	10°	15°	20°	25°	30°
S	5	32	27	22	16	11	6	0	-5	-10	-15	-21	-26	-31	-36
P	10	22	16	10	3	-3	-9	-15	-22	-27	-34	-40	-46	-52	-58
E	15	16	9	2	-5	-11	-18	-25	-31	-38	-45	-51	-58	-65	-72
E	20	12	4	-3	-10	-17	-24	-31	-39	-46	-53	-60	-67	-74	-81
D	25	8	1	-7	-15	-22	-29	-36	-44	-51	-59	-66	-74	-81	-88
	30	6	-2	-10	-18	-25	-33	-41	-49	-56	-64	-71	-79	-86	-93
	35	4	-4	-12	-20	-27	-35	-43	-52	-58	-67	-74	-82	-89	-97

Centigrade

Can you discover from this chart how cold it will be if the outside temperature is 25° and the wind is blowing 25 miles per hour? If you answered -7°, you are absolutely right! Try some other combinations.

C A T C H A C L U E

If you train your eyes on Mt. Washington in New Hampshire, you just might be able to see the very first one of its kind in the U.S. and all of North America. It's a
(a) swinging rope bridge
(b) observation tower
(c) cog railway
(answer: (c); clue: train = railway)

During the sunshine days of summer, kids can innertube, swim, canoe, and kayak in streams and rivers. Exciting little treasures can be found at country fairs, auctions, carnivals, and festivals. Every summer weekend in New Hampshire bustles with activity.

RHODE ISLAND

C O L O R   A M E R I C A !

Roses are red, but are violets really blue like the poem says? Rhode Island's violets are . . . well, many of them are violet, and they are the state flower. How do you think Rhode Island would look the color violet on your America! map?

Little Rhody and the *Ocean State* are both nicknames that describe our country's smallest state. Roger Williams was a hero, and Anne Hutchinson was a champion of religious freedom here. Newport is world famous for its music festivals and the America's Cup race. The nation's oldest Baptist church, oldest Quaker meetinghouse, and the oldest Jewish synagogue are still standing in Rhode Island. It's the smallest state in size but one of the biggest in colonial history and patriotism.

HIP, HIP, HOORAY!

If someone gave you a Rhode Island Red would you be holding an apple, a flower? Its feet might tickle your hands, but you'd be holding the state bird . . . a chicken!

PICTURE THIS

Pretend you are putting a puzzle together and you are missing 36 pieces (islands) which are scattered to the east of the state. The shape of Rhode Island looks like an unfinished puzzle, but only on the ocean side. You'll be able to find Rhode Island faster than you can say Pawtucket, Woonasquatucket, or Pettaquamscutt, three Rhode Island rivers!

Pawtucket
Providence
Scituate Reservoir
Arcadia State Park
North Kingston
Narragansett
Newport
Block Island

MAP TALK

An *island* is a body of land completely surrounded by water. It is smaller than a continent. Can you name our Pacific island state? And what about the largest island in the world? Be careful! Australia is a continent.

THE CURIOUS W's

 Who? No peeking . . . but do you know whose picture is on the one-dollar bill? I do because I'm Gilbert Stuart from North Kingston, and I'm the artist who painted the president's portrait that you see on the dollar. Who was my famous subject?
(answer: George Washington)

What? Where would you build a mansion, if you were a millionaire? Many famous American millionaires built beautiful mansions in this city on Narragansett Bay and Rhode Island Sound. These stately homes have fancy names like The Breakers, Rosecliff, The Elms, and Belcourt Castle. What's the name of this city?
(answer: Newport)

Where? Ships crashed into it, and smugglers used it as a hideaway. Cliffs of clay named Mohegan Bluffs tower up to 200' above the sea. During one shipwreck, a cow swam from the wreckage to the island and landed in a cove that is named Cow Cove. (The cow was fine.) Where is Block Island?
(answer: 10 miles south of the mainland)

Why? I was smuggled out of England wearing a disguise because skilled craftsmen weren't allowed to leave the country. I'm Samuel Slater, and when I arrived in America, I started Slater Mill. Why is my cotton mill in Pawtucket, an American milestone?
(answer: It started America's Industrial Revolution.)

Make a movie in your mind. Picture a small *island* that you can hold in your hand. On the island is a tiny *road*. A little *pro*-football player is running down the road with a *dunce* cap on his head instead of a football helmet. Road + island = Rhode Island. Pro + dunce = Providence. Providence is the capital of Rhode Island, and now you know the capital of our smallest state.

LIGHTS, CAMERA, ACTION!

Yankee Molasses Candy

Candy-making parties were popular social events in the colonies, and this recipe was used by American families during the time of the Revolutionary War.

Here's what you need:

1½	**cups light-colored molasses**
¾	**cup sugar**
1	**tablespoon vinegar**
1	**tablespoon butter**
⅛	**teaspoon baking soda**
⅛	**teaspoon salt**

Here's what you do:

1. Combine the molasses, sugar, and vinegar.
2. With an adult, cook to hard-ball stage or crisp stage (when a small amount, if dropped in a cup of very cold water, turns into a ball).
3. Add the butter, baking soda, and salt. Remove from heat, and stir until everything is blended.
4. Quickly pour onto a buttered platter or pan.
5. When cool (don't burn your fingers!), pull between buttered fingers, until candy turns white and stiff.
6. Cut into pieces. Enjoy!

CATCH A CLUE

No kidding! Can you believe that 17,000 torpedoes, made mostly by women during World War II, were made at the Naval Torpedo Station on
(a) Block Island
(b) Goat Island
(c) Prudence Island
(answer: (b); clue: kidding = Goat)

WHO SAID THAT? Have you ever felt so good about accomplishing something that you just had to tell somebody? Naval commander Oliver Hazard Perry did, too. After the American Navy fought the British on Lake Erie during a battle of the War of 1812, commander Perry said, "We have met the enemy and they are ours." He was right. The Americans won!

C O L O R   A M E R I C A !

The Green Mountain State with its Green Mountains stretching right down the middle of the state from top to bottom, and Ethan Allen and the Green Mountain Boys all suggest the same color. How about coloring Vermont on your America! map a lush shade of green?

Over 800 ski trails for snow bunnies and super stars are tucked away in Vermont's Green Mountains. The French called the area *vert* and *mont* which means green mountain, and thus the nickname, the *Green Mountain State.* The Algonquin Indians came first and then their rivals, the Iroquois. Ethan Allen and the Green Mountain Boys are state heroes. Two U.S. Presidents, Chester A. Arthur and Calvin Coolidge, were born here. Vermont is a beautiful state with an exciting and historic past.

DID YOU KNOW?

What makes Vermont's sugar maple leaves turn bright red in the fall? It's the sugar in the sap. In fact, it's this same chemical that makes maple sap sweet.

PICTURE THIS

You're holding the bottom of the state of Vermont in your hand just like the Statue of Liberty holding her torch. In fact, look closely and you'll be able to imagine Vermont as a torch. If you were to light the torch, the flames would touch Canada. Can you picture this?

WHAT A SURPRISE!

Lee, who? Have you ever heard of the word "lee"? It is the side of a mountain that is sheltered from the wind. In a storm, head for the leeward side, of course!

EARTH TALK

How could the skeleton of a whale possibly be found in Charlotte? Check out the map and see if you can solve the mystery. Remember that millions of years ago the area was covered by glaciers. Now, that's an excellent clue!

THE CURIOUS W's

Who? The Green Mountain Boys and I slipped into Fort Ticonderoga, New York, before day-break one morning. The British were still sleeping and we took the fort without a fight. We fought for Vermont's property and also for America's freedom. Who am I?
(answer: Ethan Allen)

What? Someone owed Justin Morgan some money, but he took a colt as payment, instead. Justin Morgan's horse became the father

of America's first own breed of horses. What's the name of Morgan's horses?
(answer: the Justin Morgan horse (of course!) at the Morgan Horse Farm, Weybridge)

Where? It comes from a quarry, and it was used to build some of the grandest buildings in our nation such as the Lincoln Memorial, in Washington, D.C. What is this material that comes from Danby, Dorset, and Isle La Motte?
(answer: marble)

Why? Made out of granite and towering 302' high, it's one of the tallest monuments in the world. It's the Bennington Battle Monument. The British were defeated in Bennington by an inexperienced Continental Army. Why was this victory important to the Americans?
(answer: It gave them hope that they might be able to defeat the British.)

Make a movie in your mind. Picture two mountains right next to each other. Now, picture yourself in a blizzard on the mountain on your left. *Burrrr* . . . it's cold! You're on a *mount*ain and you're saying, "Burrrr." Burrrr + mount = Vermont. The sun is shining on the other *mount*ain and when you get there you *peel* off your jacket, mittens, and hat because you're so hot. Mount + peel = Montpelier. Remember the two mountains (mounts) and you won't forget Montpelier, Vermont.

▪▪▪▪▪ Who's the "Champ"? ▪▪▪▪▪

Is there a monster lurking somewhere in the depths of Lake Champlain? Samuel de Champlain said he saw one, but that was in 1609; the story is just a legend, something like the Loch Ness monster. Champlain along with two other Frenchmen and sixty Algonquin Indians, paddled 24 canoes into Lake Champlain, where Champlain claimed the 100-mile long lake for himself! French forts and settlements lined its shores, and military battles were fought there. Today, this beautiful lake is home to fishing, water sports, and scenic boat rides. And guess what? People today still say they have seen the friendly Lake Champlain monster, affectionately known as "Champ."

Ⓒ Ⓐ Ⓣ Ⓒ Ⓗ Ⓐ Ⓒ Ⓛ Ⓤ Ⓔ

Pancakes and waffles would be sad without it. Vermont is the number one producer of maple syrup in the country. It takes an unbelievable 40 gallons of maple sap to make how many gallons of maple syrup?

(a) 5
(b) 3
(c) 1
(answer: (c); clue: one = 1)

PACK YOUR BAGS

After a winter of fun in the snow — cross-country skiing, downhill skiing, and snow-mobiling — Vermonters look forward to "sugar-on-snow." Hot maple syrup is poured over dishes of powdered snow or ice cream for a deliciously sweet treat. Guess what they eat with this to cut the sweetness? You won't believe it, but it's sour pickles! It's a Vermont tradition to brighten the days of "mud season," Vermont's "fifth season" which falls between winter and spring when the snow melts.

THE MID-ATLANTIC STATES

NAME THE CAPITAL

How many capitals of the Mid–Atlantic states can you name? Write the names below, then check your answers on the state maps. Each state capital is marked with a ✪. Did you get all five state capitals correct?

DELAWARE _____

MARYLAND _____

NEW JERSEY _____

NEW YORK _____

PENNSYLVANIA _____

For information on Washington, D.C., please see pages 166-167.

DELAWARE

Delaware is the only state to have had three European flags — the Dutch, English, and Swedish — fly over its original colony. Today, it is known as the chemical capital of the world. Picturesque and historic towns such as Lewes and New Castle remind us of Delaware's proud, historic ties to America's past. It's the second smallest state, but the first to ratify the Constitution of the United States and the only state that has a boundary formed by the arc of a perfect circle. Delaware is truly the *First State*.

MAP TALK

One Time Around: A sphere has 360 degrees. What number do you get when you divide 15 into 360? You're right! It's 24.

How many hours in a day? 24, right again!

Guess how many time zones there are in the world? Would you believe 24?

Can you figure out how many hours in each time zone? Divide 24 by 24. What did you get? One hour.

How many hours does it take for the earth to make one complete turn on its axis? What do you know, it's 24 hours! Here's the toughest question of all. How many degrees out of the 360 is one hour? Ah, you peeked at the first part of the question. It's 15°.

There are 24 separate 15° segments of one hour each around the earth. These segments are known as time zones. What time zone do you live in?

Wilmington

First Log Cabin

Pea Patch Island

Dover

Milford

Lewes

Rehoboth Beach

Trap Pond State Park

COLOR AMERICA!

You've heard of the story book characters, the Little Red Hen and Henny Penny, but Delaware has the real thing. Its state bird is the Blue Hen Chicken. Pick your favorite shade of blue to color Delaware on your America! map. Blue Hen Chickens will be proud.

HIP, HIP, HOORAY!

A five star salute to the five members of the Bayard family of Delaware who have served as United States senators starting with James who began serving at the close of the War of 1812. No other family in our country has equalled this family's Senate record. Hip, Hip, Hooray!

PICTURE THIS

I spy. How can you look straight ahead and see what's behind you? You can do it with a periscope. Look at Delaware as if you were on a submarine in the Atlantic Ocean. The bottom of the state is the view finder, and if you follow the state all the way to the top it looks like a periscope spying on New Jersey which is behind you. Periscope up!

THE CURIOUS W's

 Who? During the early 1800s, gunpowder was of such poor quality that I started a gun powder plant. This was the beginning of our family's chemical company that became the largest in the world. Have you heard of cellophane, Nylon, Teflon, and polyester? My initials are E.I. Do you know my family's name?
(answer: du Pont; Wilmington)

 What? What could possibly be pounded by the ocean and still grow taller every year as the ocean pushes more and more sand upon it? It's over 100 feet high and has even been known to swallow trees as it piles upward and inland. What is this landmark?
(answer: a sand dune called Great Sand Hill; near Lewes)

 Where? A very strange thing happened many years ago in the Delaware River, or so they say. A cargo ship carrying peas was wrecked on a sandbar, spilling the peas into the river. They sprouted, snagging debris along with more sand, and eventually built up to form an island! This island is called, to no one's surprise, Pea Patch Island! Can you find this on the map?

 Why? When the Swedes settled in Delaware, they built their homes out of logs rather than boards or planks. Other settlers began to copy this design. Why was this know-how important to America?
(answer: It introduced the log cabin; northern Delaware)

 Delaware's coastline has wonderful beaches, and during the summertime, Rehoboth Beach is so filled with government officials and their families, it is nicknamed the "Nation's Summer Capital."

 Make a movie in your mind. Wouldn't it be a funny sight to see a *doe* (female deer) walking into a *deli wearing a fur* jacket? Imagine her ordering a corned beef sandwich! Deli + wear = Delaware and Doe + fur = Dover. Dover, Delaware, you've got it!

—————The JELLO™ State —————

JELLO™ and Delaware go together (it was first made there), and this recipe is so easy and tasty that you just might want a sweet reminder of Delaware often. *Here's what you need*: 3 small packages of sugar-free JELLO™, 4 envelopes unflavored gelatin, 4 cups boiling water. *Here's what you do*: Mix the JELLO™, unflavored gelatin, and boiling water until completely dissolved. Pour into a 9" x 12" pan and chill until firm. Now, gently draw the shape of Delaware into the gelatin. You can cut it out and move your state to a separate platter or mark the outline with a squiggle of whipped cream. Mark some of the places you want to remember about Delaware with pieces of fruit or mini-marshmallows. Isn't it Del-icious!

WHAT A WASTE!

Ninety thousand pounds of trash are thrown away in the typical lifetime of each American.

IT MAKES CENTS

 You can earn some spare cash - not to mention a great feeling — every time you recycle. Ask at the supermarket if you can have three cardboard boxes. Label one newspapers, one aluminum cans, and one glass bottles. Separate your trash and turn it in at your neighborhood recycling center. If you want to help America and the Planet Earth, start in your own neighborhood today!

MARYLAND

Have you ever seen a black-eyed Susan? It looks like a large yellow daisy. And, did you know that the Baltimore oriole is yellow, black, and white? Maryland's state flower is the black-eyed Susan, and the Oriole is the state bird.

Knights in shining armor charging with lances ride their mounts in jousting festivals in Maryland. Why? Because jousting is the state's official sport! But lacrosse, the Preakness horse race, and the Baltimore Orioles of baseball's American League are also part of Maryland's sporting attractions. Civil War nurse, Clara Barton, is honored as the founder of the American Red Cross, and Maryland is home to Camp David, the official presidential retreat. The Allegheny River and Blue Ridge Mountains add to the picturesque beauty of the *Old Line State*, enhanced by the famous Potomac River and Chesapeake Bay.

Antietam

Potomac River

Baltimore
Fort McHenry
Annapolis

Ocean City

CHESAPEAKE BAY

A little yellow from both the flower and the bird might be just the right color for Maryland on your America! map.

PICTURE THIS

You'll really have to use your imagination on this one, but if you'll look closely, picture Maryland as a prehistoric bird. The bird is flying toward the west with both wings flapping down. The space between the wings is the Chesapeake Bay. Can you see the head and beak heading west? That's a funny looking bird!

THE CURIOUS W's

Who? The "Sultan of Swat" and "King of Swing" were two of my nicknames. I was a left-handed pitcher, but I became famous as a hitter. I held the all-time home run record of 714 until Hank Aaron broke the record in 1974. Who am I?
(answer: George Herman "Babe" Ruth; Baltimore)

What? Young men and women receive commissions as a Navy ensign or a Marine second lieutenant when they graduate from this college. President Jimmy Carter is the only U.S. President to have graduated from this famous American school. What is its name?
(answer: United States Naval Academy; Annapolis)

Where? The Chesapeake Bay is an inlet. In fact, it's the largest inlet on the Atlantic Coast. Maryland's largest river, the Potomac, empties into this bay. Can you locate the Chesapeake Bay which is home to many excellent Maryland ports?

 Why? Frances Scott Key couldn't believe it when he saw that the American flag was still flying over Fort McHenry, which had been bombarded throughout the night by the British fleet during a battle of the War of 1812. Why is the battle at Fort McHenry important to our heritage?
(answer: Francis Scott Key wrote a poem that became the words to our national anthem after this battle.)

 LIGHTS, CAMERA, ACTION!

Make a movie in your mind. Picture yourself at a wedding. You see a beautiful bride dangling an *apple* from a fishing *pole*, but she's trying to hook her groom, not a fish! She really wants to *land* this live one and get *married*. Now you know the capital of Maryland. An apple + pole = Annapolis. Married + land = Maryland. Ring those wedding bells in Annapolis, Maryland!

 **HOW'S YOUR LATITUDE ATTITUDE?**

Are Annapolis, Maryland and Athens, Greece on the same approximate latitude (38°N) as Detroit, Michigan or Reno, Nevada?

PACK YOUR BAGS

Jet-skiing, parasailing, windsurfing, waterskiing, surfboarding, and sailing sound like things to do in Hawaii, but Ocean City also offers all of these exciting water sports during vacation months. After a day at the boardwalk and beach, saddle up and mosey on down to the Wild, Wild West at the Eastern Shore theme park where old-time gunfights and bank robberies happen every day. Stagecoach, riverboat, train, and pony rides all make for family fun.

MAP TALK

To a Degree: Latitudes are measured in degrees, beginning at the equator. The equator is 0° latitude. It is 90° from the equator to the North Pole and 90° from the equator to the South Pole. When we talk about latitudes, a location is always north or south of the equator, or directly on the equator. Don't forget, it's about 70 miles between each degree of latitude, so if you were 5° latitude north of the equator, you would be 350 miles north. Still pretty hot, huh!

DID YOU KNOW?

Have you read the book, *Misty of Chincoteague*? Chincoteague ponies are real wild ponies that live on Assateague Island. When a Spanish galleon was shipwrecked sometime in the 16th century, the ancestors of these ponies swam ashore, and they've been there ever since.

A SUPREME COURT WINNER

As a lawyer he brought 32 cases to the U.S. Supreme Court, and he won 29 of them. His most important was the case which he argued against the segregation of blacks in our schools. He won the decision. Thurgood Marshall, born in Baltimore, is the only black person, until his retirement in June of 1991, to ever serve as a Supreme Court associate justice. The great-grandson of a slave, Justice Marshall was a great crusader for racial equality and individual human rights. He retired from the court at age 82 after serving for 24 years, and he's honored by all Americans for his courageous support of civil and personal rights.

Cold Floors - Warm Ceilings

The further you live from the equator, the colder it gets. Saving energy is important and it's a lot easier when you understand a basic heat fact: it rises! Let's experiment at your kitchen sink.

Here's what you need:

2 identical pint jars, 2 index cards, and some food coloring.

Here's what you do:

1. Fill one jar with cold water and the other with warm water.

2. Put a few drops of food coloring in the jar of warm water and set it in the empty sink.

3. Place the index card over the top of the cold water jar, turn it upside down, and place it on top of the warm water jar. It's kind of tricky.

4. Gently pull the card from between the two jars and watch what happens to the warm, colored water. It mixes together with the cold, right?

5. Now, empty the jars and reverse the experiment by putting the warm, colored water in the top jar and the cold, clear water in the bottom jar.

6. Remove the card and watch what happens. Surprise! Cold and warm do not mix when the warm water begins in the top jar.

Now that you understand that heat rises, how can you start saving energy?

HIP, HIP, HOORAY!

When General Stonewall Jackson and his troops marched through Frederick, Maryland, Barbara Fritchie, who was 90 years old at the time, was flying the Union flag. When Jackson ordered the flag shot down, Fritchie reportedly said, "Shoot, if you must, this old gray head, but spare your country's flag." When she grabbed the flag, Jackson told his men to hold their fire. This is how the story goes according to John Greenleaf Whittier, who wrote a poem about what happened. Hooray for Barbara Fritchie, and three cheers for Stonewall Jackson!

WHO SAID THAT?

When American naval officer, John Paul Jones, was asked to surrender during a great Revolutionary War sea battle against the British, he said, "I have not yet begun to fight!" His ship, the Bonhomme Richard, was sinking, but Jones meant what he said. The Americans went on to win the battle!

NEW JERSEY

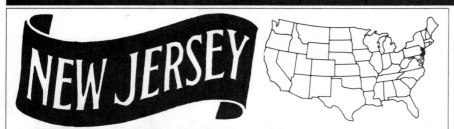

What do you imagine growing in a garden? Plenty of fresh vegetables like lettuce or carrots? Maybe you see beautiful flowers and green-leafed plants. New Jersey is the *Garden State* so color your America! map the colors of your imaginary (or real) garden. What color did you choose?

With the Atlantic Ocean as a setting, New Jersey has a variety of unusual beach towns from Sandy Hook to Cape May. Its 127-mile shoreline is famous for its wonderful beaches, boardwalks, hotels, and casinos. Forests, farms, industrial cities, lowlands, and marshes complete its varied landscape. New Jersey is truly a melting pot of cultures, businesses, industry, and people who love the state's diversity and character. Say "hello" to the *Garden State!*

Getting Ready: You hear it on the news, you read about it in the newspapers, and you may talk about it in your science class. What is it? It's the *greenhouse effect.* You may already know that a greenhouse is a glass or heavy plastic structure where plants grow in a controlled heat and humidity environment. What do you think it means when we hear that the earth is experiencing the greenhouse effect? What might happen where you live if the earth gradually became warmer? Think about it.

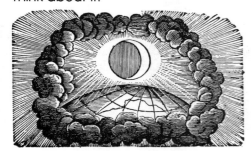

High Point State Park

Paterson

★ West Orange

Newark

Sandy Hook

Trenton ⊛

Asbury Park

Camden

Atlantic City

Cape May

PICTURE THIS

Can this be true? Kids throwing their socks on the bedroom floor? Nonsense. It's probably just a rumor started by parents, but if that ever did happen, picture New Jersey as a sock that has just been dropped. Notice how it bends. The top of the sock touches New York, and the other end is on Delaware. Take a look.

HIP, HIP, HOORAY!

When Mary McCauley's husband collapsed from the unbearable heat during a Revolutionary War battle, she took over his position and helped fire the cannon! She also brought water from a nearby spring to the soldiers. The men would cry out to her, "Molly, the pitcher." From then on, Mary McCauley was known as Molly Pitcher. What a great American patriot!

THE CURIOUS W's

Who? My mother said that I loved to ask questions, and I also liked to find out how things worked. My favorite invention was the phonograph, but inventing the electric light was also exciting. Who am I?
(answer: Thomas Alva Edison; West Orange)

What? This wooden structure is perfect for walking and people-watching. You'll also find ice cream parlors, cafes, souvenir shops, fast-food restaurants, arcades, and amusement parks here. There are several of these in New Jersey's beach cities, but the best known is in Atlantic City. What am I?
(answer: a boardwalk)

Why? General George Washington and his troops crossed the icy Delaware River one night in 1776. Why is this considered to be a brilliant military maneuver?
(answer: The Americans surprised the enemy soldiers who were busy celebrating Christmas. They took nearly 1,000 prisoners in this great victory of the Revolutionary War.)

Make a movie in your mind. Picture your favorite football player taking a brand new jersey off, laying it on the floor, and stretching it. Now he places a *tent on* the *new jersey*. You've just learned the capital of New Jersey. Tent on = Trenton and new jersey = New Jersey. Trenton, New Jersey. Wow!

WHAT STATE IS YOUR GARDEN IN?

New Jersey is known as the Garden State for good reason — its fertile land has long encouraged truck farmers to grow luscious crops that they bring to market in the big cities such as New York. But you don't have to be a truck farmer or even have an outdoor space to grow some great food and flowers of your own. *Here's what you need for a container garden*: a large container such as a flowerbox, planter, wooden box, or several coffee cans; potting soil; some stones or pebbles; water and sunshine (a sunny window sill will do just fine!); a few seedlings or seeds. *Here's what you do*: Select what you want to grow. Herbs like parsley and chives, a bush cherry tomato plant, radishes, flowers like geraniums and impatience all do well indoors. Poke a few drainage holes in the bottom of your container and then line it with pebbles. Fill with rich soil. Plant your seedlings so that their roots have plenty of room to spread out, or plant your seeds according to directions (not too deep). Set in sun and water so that the soil is moist, but not wet. No matter where you live you can find some plant that will grow with your love and attention!

C A T C H A C L U E

Were there college ball games in America in 1869? Yes! Rutgers beat Princeton 6 to 4 in the first game of its kind in the U.S. Name that sport.
(a) soccer
(b) rugby
(c) football
(answer: (c); clue: ball = football)

What do Boardwalk, Atlantic Avenue, Marvin Gardens, and Park Place remind you of? Why, it's the celebrated board game, Monopoly! And guess where all of those street names come from? You guessed it — Atlantic City, New Jersey. If you guessed right, go past "Go" and collect $200; otherwise, go directly to "Jail"!

Over 8,000 sparkling lakes and rivers, the majestic Adirondack Mountains, and rolling hills give New York state a rich, scenic beauty that makes the *Empire State* one of our nation's favorite vacationlands. Resorts, parks, and historic forts enhance the state's landscape. Did Peter Minuit really buy Manhattan Island from the Native Americans for only $24 worth of trinkets? Today, New York City is filled with history and places that make it America's most famous city and also our most populated. From its colonial beginnings to the glitter of Broadway, sports, cultural arts, high finance, manufacturing, and business, NYC is unmatched.

The "Big Apple" is what New York City is called by many people. Have you ever wondered why? Do you suppose it could be because it's such a big city and because the state's fruit is an apple? Golden delicious and pippins are apples that are a rich yellow color. How about coloring New York on your America! map yellow for the "Big Apple" and for those juicy yellow apples?

LAKE ONTARIO

Alexandria Bay

Fort Ticonderoga

Adirondack State Park

Niagara Falls

Buffalo

LAKE ERIE

Rochester

Syracuse

Utica

Finger Lakes Region

Corning

Albany

Catskill Mts.

Kingston

Hudson River

New York City

Long Island

Ellis Island

PICTURE THIS

It's a seal! The northeast corner is the nose that could be balancing a red apple. Check out Long Island in the Atlantic Ocean and see if you can picture it as the seal's flippers. Can you see the body and the tail? This seal does have a large head, but if you look closely you can almost hear it barking! The red apple he's balancing will remind you that the apple is the state fruit!

THE CURIOUS W's

 Who? I started out poor, but ended up a millionaire. I made my fortune in the oil business, and during my lifetime, I gave over $600 million away to schools, charities, and foundations. I have a very famous Fifth Avenue center in New York City named after me. Who am I?
(answer: John D. Rockefeller, Rockefeller Center)

 What? I was a gift to America from France, and at 305 feet from my pedestal to the torch in my right hand, I'm very tall for a lady. You can find me overlooking New York Harbor. I celebrated my 100th birthday in 1986, and my party was wonderful. What am I?
(answer: The Statue of Liberty)

 Where? Daredevils have illegally tumbled over it in barrels, but you can ride beneath me in the boat, the Maid of the Mist. It's 184 feet of cascading, crashing, thundering water known as Niagara Falls. Where am I?
(answer: Northwest corner of New York across the border from Ontario, Canada)

 Why? A butcher owned these 27 acres that were known by such names as Bucking, Oyster, and Gull, before the government bought this land from him. It's name was then changed to Ellis Island, and this became one of America's most important sites. Do you know why?
(answer: 20 million immigrants passed through the processing center here before starting a new life in America)

 Make a movie in your mind. Picture a very tall building. What is that building? It's the *Empire State Building* in New York City, and you see animals with long ears jumping around all over the building. What are those animals? They're *all bunnies*. You've just learned the capital of New York. All bunnies = Albany. Empire State Building = New York. Albany, New York. Hippety-hop!

- - - - - C - A - M - P - - - - -

Our North American Neighbors: Plan a camp-out with our North American neighbors, and you'll never forget who they are. Starting with Canada at 12 o'clock, picture a capital letter C. At 3 o'clock is a capital letter A for the Atlantic Ocean. At 6 o'clock we have a capital letter M for Mexico, and at 9 o'clock there's a capital letter P for the Pacific Ocean. What do the 4 letters spell? C-A-M-P = camp; *Canada, the Atlantic Ocean, Mexico, the Pacific Ocean.* Can you remember our neighbors by thinking of the word camp and picturing camping out with our closest friends — two countries and two oceans?

MAP TALK

ⒸⒶⓉⒸⒽ Ⓐ ⒸⓁⓊⒺ

With Indian names of Cayuga, Seneca, and Owasko, the number of these celebrated, long narrow lakes can be counted on your fingers. They're called
(a) Great Lakes
(b) Lake of the Woods
(c) Finger Lakes
(answer: (c); clue: fingers = Finger)

NEW YORK

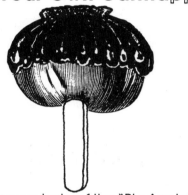

Make Your Own Carmapples?

You can have a taste of the "Big Apple" without hopping a plane or getting into a car. Just try these easy-to-do caramel covered apples. They're mouth-watering.

Here's what you need: 6 medium apples, one 14 oz. bag of caramels, wooden sticks, waxed paper, and perhaps, chopped peanuts or other nuts.

Here's what you do: Poke a stick into the stem end of the washed and dried apples. Unwrap the caramels and place in a saucepan with 3 tablespoons of water. Heat over very low heat until the mixture is well-blended. Remove from heat and dip each apple into the mixture, turning to coat completely, using a spoon if necessary. Hold the apple upright for a few seconds before placing the stick side up on waxed paper. If you want to cover with nuts, wait a few seconds before rolling it in the chopped nuts. What else could you roll the apples in? How about miniature chocolate chips, granola, raisins, crunchy cereal, or — you name it!

HOME OF HEROES

Some of baseball's greatest heroes played for the New York Yankees. Super stars like Babe Ruth, Lou Gehrig, Joe DiMaggio, Mickey Mantle, and Roger Maris made the Yankees the legends of baseball. And what about the Dodgers? Did you know that they were affectionately called Brooklyn's "bums," before they moved to L.A.? Jackie Robinson made sports' history when he joined the Dodgers and became the first black person to play major league baseball.

Baseball great, Willie Mays was a New York Giant, before that team moved to San Francisco in 1957. Then along came those "Amazing Mets." The new team in town captured three World Series championships. New York still has its Yankees and Mets, and Yankee Stadium and Shea Stadium continue to pack 'em in! "Play ball!"

HOME, AT LAST

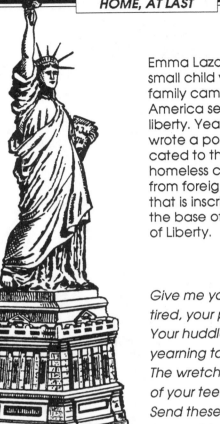

Emma Lazarus was a small child when her family came to America seeking liberty. Years later she wrote a poem dedicated to the tired and homeless coming from foreign shores that is inscribed on the base of the Statue of Liberty.

*Give me your
tired, your poor,
Your huddled masses
yearning to breathe free,
The wretched refuse
of your teeming shore.
Send these, the homeless,
tempest-tost to me,
I lift my lamp beside
the golden door!*

HIP, HIP, HOORAY!

"Smile!" "Watch the birdie," and "Say cheese" were what George Eastman liked to hear. He loved photography even when he was a kid, so do you know what he did? He figured out how to make film that could be wound on a roller, but that's not all. By 1900 his company was making cameras that sold for one dollar each, and guess what he named his famous camera? The Kodak!

PACK YOUR BAGS

With all the interest in baseball in New York, it's no wonder that Cooperstown has the Baseball Hall of Fame. If you were traveling from upstate New York down to NYC, you might want to visit the United States Military Academy at West Point, and stop in at Bear Mountain State Park, too. Of course, you could spend a month of Sundays in NYC, where you would certainly want to visit the United Nations Headquarters and the World Trade Center, before heading off to Central Park, Jones Beach, the Bronx Zoo, and Coney Island (for their famous hot dogs). Kids and grown-ups never run out of things to see and do in New York state!

WHO SAID THAT?

"The only thing we have to fear is fear itself" is what President Franklin D. Roosevelt told the American people. He said this to encourage the many people who had lost their jobs and couldn't find work. Do you think this was good advice?

PENNSYLVANIA

COLOR AMERICA!

Three cheers for the red, white, and blue! What do those colors bring to mind? The American flag, and when we think of the flag who comes to mind? Why Betsy Ross, who was born in Pennsylvania. Would you like to color Pennsylvania red, white, and blue on your America! map? Three cheers if you do!

Charles II, King of England, owed money to William Penn's father. The enormous estate (over 28 million acres) of wooded land given to the younger Penn as payment of that debt became Pennsylvania, known as the *Keystone State* because of its key importance to the 13 colonies. Home of the first fire department, first hospital, first lending library, and the first fire insurance company in America, Philadelphia became the leading city of colonial life. The signing of the Declaration of Independence and the United States Constitution in Philadelphia has etched Pennsylvania in our nation's heritage forever.

Erie

Hills Creek State Park

Parker Dam State Park

Black Moshannon State Park

Susquehanna River

Scranton

Appalachian Mts.

Pittsburgh

Bethlehem

Valley Forge

Harrisburg

Gettysburg

Philadelphia

PICTURE THIS

A big fat fish with its mouth open wide is what Pennsylvania looks like. You can even see part of its little fish tail sticking up at the northwest corner. The fish must be heading for the open waters of the Atlantic Ocean, after it gobbles up New Jersey to its east.

 Make a movie in your mind. You're a cartoonist, and you're drawing some cartoon character *hairy hamburgers* with your yellow *pencil*. When you think of Pennsylvania think of a pencil, and when you think of the weird hairy burgers, you can remember Harrisburg which is the capital of Pennsylvania. Pencil = Pennsylvania and hairy burger = Harrisburg. Harrisburg, Pennsylvania. Now for the bald hot dogs!

THE CURIOUS W's

 Who? George Washington made the rough sketch, but he wanted the stars to be six pointed! I talked him into the five-pointed version, and then I made the first official American flag in 1776. I bet you know who I am.
(answer: Betsy Ross; Philadelphia)

 What? This 2,000 pound bell was one that rang out from churches all around Philadelphia on July 8, 1776 to proclaim the adoption of the Declaration of Independence. Years later, it was cracked beyond repair while ringing to celebrate George Washington's birthday. Can you name this grand symbol of freedom?
(answer: Liberty Bell; Philadelphia)

 Where? Over 3,000 soldiers died here. Smallpox, the bitter cold, and scarce food and clothing ended the lives of these valiant patriots. On December 23, 1777, George Washington wrote, "We have this day no less than 2,973 men in camp unfit for duty, because they are barefoot and otherwise naked." The place? Valley Forge. Can you find this site?

 Why? Gettysburg was the scene of the greatest battle ever fought in the Western hemisphere. It was the turning point of the Civil War, which the Union went on to win. It was also the scene of one of the most famous speeches ever given by a U.S. President. Do you know who gave that speech and what it was called?
(answer: Abraham Lincoln; the Gettysburg Address)

PENNSYLVANIA

Weather or Not!

Lightning streaked across the blackened sky. Thunder rumbled in the distance. It wasn't the kind of day you should ever pick to fly a kite, but Ben and his son, William, were about to make history. On the outskirts of Philadelphia, the two stood in a shed to keep the end of the string dry, when suddenly a bolt of lightning flashed and lit up the sky. Thunder rolled across the hills, and electricity shot from the wire on top of the kite to the iron key at the end of the string. Ben touched the key and an electric shock shook his body. Lightning and electricity were the same thing! Ben Franklin shocked the world with this important discovery.

WHO SAID THAT?

"Fish and visitors smell in three days,"
"A small leak will sink a great ship," and
"Early to bed and early to rise makes a man healthy, wealthy and wise," are all sayings that Ben Franklin wrote in his *Poor Richard's Almanac.* And don't forget, "A penny saved is a penny earned!"

PACK YOUR BAGS

There's so much to do and see in Pennsylvania, you'll wonder how anyone ever gets any work done! It might take your breath away, but oh, what a ride you'll take at Eaglesmere Lake. The journey propels you down a 1,200 foot toboggan run, zooming along at over 40 miles per hour. Are you game for this one? If you can say "Youghiogheny," you can probably keep your seat in a boat on that river's white water rapids. For calmer days, head out to Pennsylvania Dutch and Amish country around Lancaster, and don't miss the tour of the Hershey Chocolate Factory (with delicious samples). Be sure to visit Gettysburg and take the Lackawana Mine tour in Ashland. Most of all — have fun!

--- GO FLY A KITE ---

Ben Franklin did, but how would you like to try something really different? Here's directions for a very unique, easy-to-make, easy-to-fly kite. When you make this, you may even come up with a better design of your own. Give it a try, and don't forget to decorate the paper first. Be daring!

Here's what you need:

> 3 plastic drinking straws, 2 pieces of 8½" x 11" paper, white glue, tape, kite string or thread.

Here's what you do:

1. Place the paper in front of you with the short side at the top.

2. Place one straw across the top of your paper. Fold the paper over the straw and glue it down. Place one straw at the bottom of your paper. Fold over and glue, just like you did on top.

3. Tape the third straw in the center of the paper, going up and down.

4. When the straws are glued tightly, turn the kite over and poke two sets of holes as shown.

5. Make a bridle for the kite out of thread or string by tieing one string to the top of the center straw and one to the bottom. Tie them together (see drawing) and then attach it to your kite string.

6. Make two tails for your kite about 1-inch wide and 12-inches long from ribbon, paper, or cloth. If it's very windy, you'll need longer tails or even 3 strips. Glue tails to kite. Try it out and make adjustments. Up, up, and away!

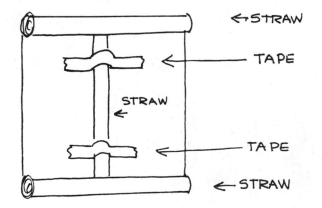

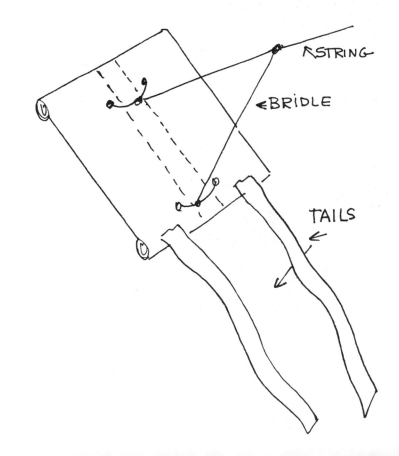

WEATHER WATCH

Flash! Boom! Have you ever wondered how close the lightning is during a thunderstorm? Here's a hint: Count one chimpanzee, two chimpanzees, three chimpanzees, and so on, until you hear the boom. For every five chimpanzees you say, the lightning is one mile away. 5 chimpanzees = 1 mile away; 10 chimpanzees = 2 miles away. Can you tell how many miles away the lightning would be if you counted 15 chimpanzees? Three is absolutely right!

THE SOUTHEASTERN STATES

NAME THE CAPITAL

How many capitals of the Southeastern states can you name? Write the names below, then check your answers on the state maps. Each state capital is marked with a ✪. Did you get all six state capitals correct?

FLORIDA _____

GEORGIA _____

NORTH CAROLINA _____

SOUTH CAROLINA _____

VIRGINIA _____

WEST VIRGINIA _____

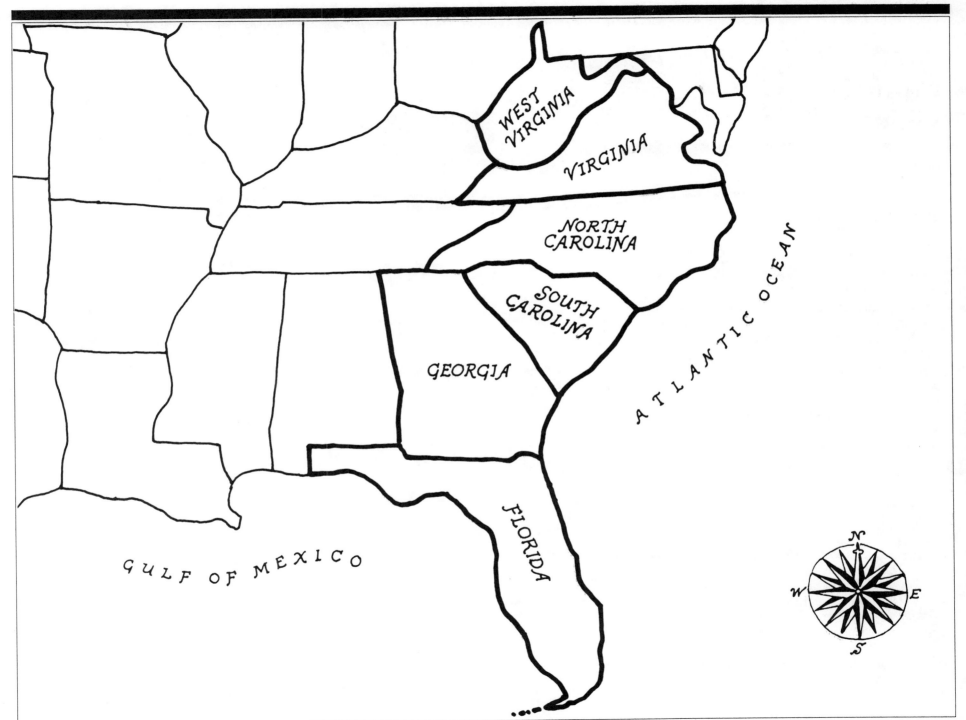

If you drink orange juice for breakfast made from frozen concentrate, you are most likely drinking the juice of Florida oranges. Most of our frozen orange juice comes from the *Sunshine State*. The orange blossom is Florida's state flower and with the Orange Bowl football game played on New Year's Day, what else could Florida be on your America! map except a luscious shade of orange.

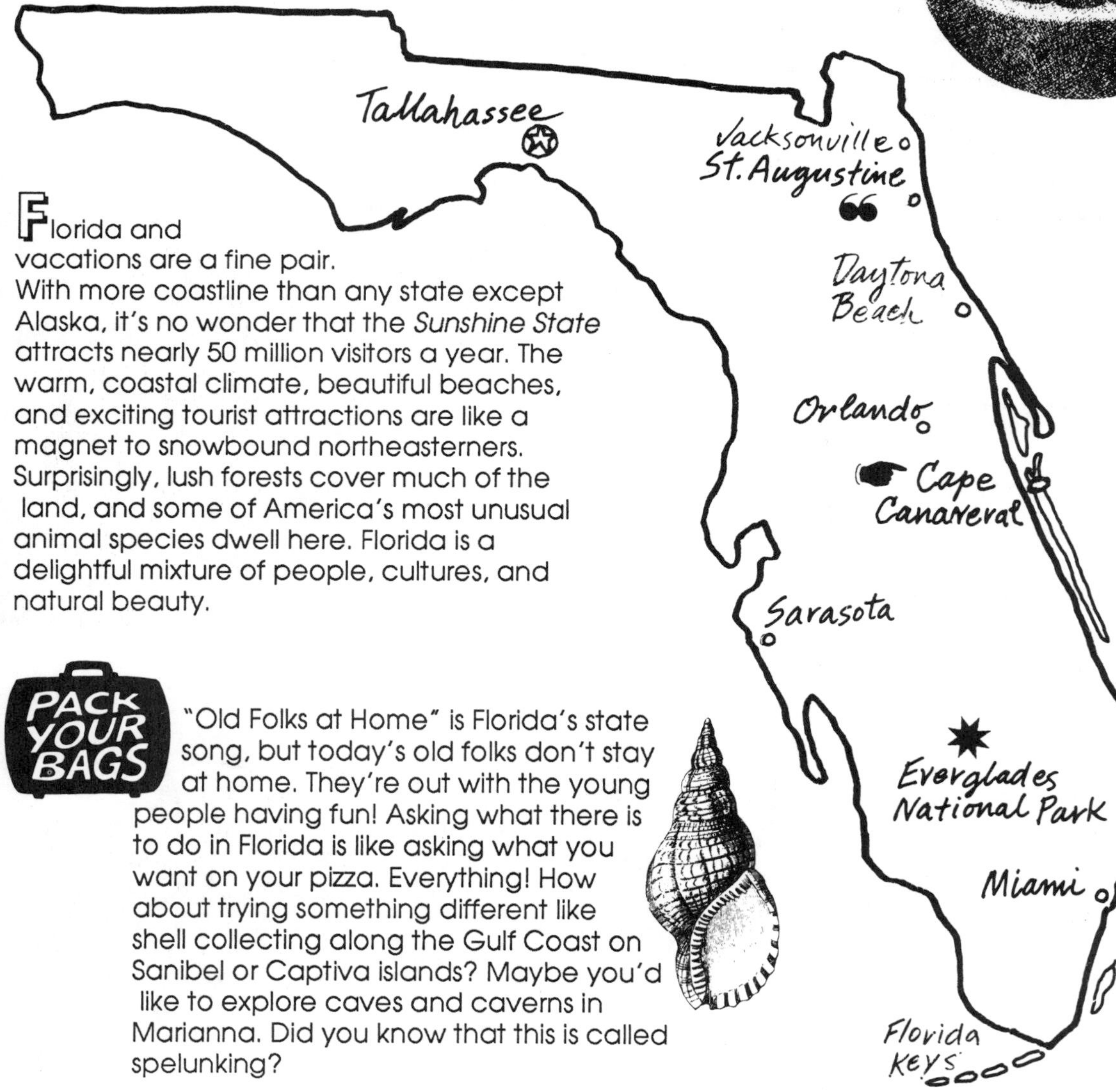

Florida and vacations are a fine pair. With more coastline than any state except Alaska, it's no wonder that the *Sunshine State* attracts nearly 50 million visitors a year. The warm, coastal climate, beautiful beaches, and exciting tourist attractions are like a magnet to snowbound northeasterners. Surprisingly, lush forests cover much of the land, and some of America's most unusual animal species dwell here. Florida is a delightful mixture of people, cultures, and natural beauty.

PACK YOUR BAGS "Old Folks at Home" is Florida's state song, but today's old folks don't stay at home. They're out with the young people having fun! Asking what there is to do in Florida is like asking what you want on your pizza. Everything! How about trying something different like shell collecting along the Gulf Coast on Sanibel or Captiva islands? Maybe you'd like to explore caves and caverns in Marianna. Did you know that this is called spelunking?

GATOR OR CROC?

If either of these famous Florida reptiles were one giant chomp away from the seat of your pants, it wouldn't matter! To settle the controversy, here's the scoop. Alligators have a broad snout that is rounded at the end, while crocodiles have a long, narrow snout that comes to a point. There are lots of alligators in Florida, but very few crocodiles.

PICTURE THIS

Picture a peninsula in the south east corner of the United States. Don't forget that a *peninsula* is land surrounded on three sides by water. This peninsula is Florida, and it looks just like a finger sticking out in the ocean. It looks like it's pointing at something. Could it be pointing at the Atlantic sailfish? That's Florida's salt water state fish.

Map labels: Tallahassee, Jacksonville, St. Augustine, Daytona Beach, Orlando, Cape Canaveral, Sarasota, Everglades National Park, Miami, Florida Keys

THE CURIOUS W's

 What? Alan B. Shepard, Jr. made the first sub-orbital space flight, and John H. Glenn was the first American to orbit the earth. Neil A. Armstrong was the first man to walk on the moon. These three historical space launches were made from the John F. Kennedy Space Center. Can you name the famous cape where these launchings took place?
(answer: Cape Canaveral; near Titusville and Cocoa Beach)

Where? "Flying carpets" and "the swamp sleds" can be seen gliding through the rugged waterways of the Everglades. Alligators, crocodiles, panthers, storks, and snowy egrets call America's third largest national park their home. Can you find Everglades National Park at the southern tip of Florida?

Why? Spanish explorer Juan Ponce de León was looking for the Fountain of Youth when he explored this area in 1513. He didn't find the spring of water that stories said could make people young again, but he named the land Florida for its beautiful flowers. Why do you suppose St. Augustine is an important historical site?
(answer: It's the oldest city in the U.S.)

CATCH A CLUE

Florida was launched into national prominence when it was the first state to
(a) breed crocodiles out of captivity
(b) make a synthetic diamond
(c) launch an earth satellite
(answer: (c); clue: launched = launch)

 **LIGHTS, CAMERA, ACTION!** Make a movie in your mind. Picture a dog doing something very unusual. He's got a towel in his mouth, and he's mopping your kitchen *floor*. Who is this talented dog with the *towel*? Why, he's none other than the famous movie star dog, *Lassie*. Floor = Florida and towel + Lassie = Tallahassee. Tallahassee, Florida!

S•T•A•T•E • S•L•A•P

Here's what you need: 100 small pieces of blank paper, pencil and paper. Write the names of each state on 50 of the pieces of paper, and write the state capitals on the other 50.
Here's what you do: Shuffle both groups of cards together and place face down on the table. First player turns the top card face up. If any player knows the answer, he tries to be the first one to slap the card. If it is a state card, "slapper" tells the capital. If it is a capital card, "slapper" tells the state name. Answer must be given in 5 seconds. "Slapper" keeps that card if answer is correct. If answer is incorrect, the card remains face up and the next drawn card goes on top of it. The next person who slaps a card and gives a correct answer picks up all the cards under it, too. Player with most cards wins the game.

 EARTH TALK

Is it possible to move when you're standing still? Remember that the earth rotates on its axis every 24 hours. The earth is approximately 25,000 miles around at the equator. About how fast do you think you are traveling right now: 10 miles per hour? 100 miles an hour? 1,000 miles per hour? You're right, it's 1,000 miles per hour. For standing still, that's going pretty fast. Hang on!

Homemade peach ice cream, peach cobbler, peach pie, or peaches and cream are all mouth-watering Georgia treats made with the state's fruit that just happens to be the peach. If you can't find a peach color for Georgia, orange with red shaded lightly over the top gives the same effect. Georgia will always stand out on your America! map, because it is the only state the color of peaches!

Ⓖone With The Wind, written in Georgia by Margaret Mitchell of Atlanta, is about the *Peach State* and life in the South. It's one of our country's most beloved and popular books and motion pictures. It depicts true southern charm and traditions along with the ravages of the Civil War. Georgia, land of mountains, rolling hills, river valleys, swamps, and coastline islands, is filled with striking natural sites, historic landmarks, and wonderful cities.

HIP, HIP, HOORAY!

Girl Scouts didn't sell cookies in 1912, but Juliet Gordon Low started the Girl Guides in Savannah in that year, and the all-girl organization was later called the Girl Scouts. Juliet Low was a true pioneering scout herself. Cheers!

MAPTALK

Hold an orange in your left hand, with your finger and thumb forming a "C" at the stem (North Pole) and the bottom (South Pole). If you traced along the C-shape from top to bottom, you would be forming a line called a *meridian*. There are 360 meridians around the whole earth. (Slowly turn the orange in your fingers and you will get the idea of how they work.) These imaginary lines are also called *longitude lines* on a map. Longitude lines go the long way on the map, up and down.

Appalachian Mts.

Atlanta

Athens

Augusta

Savannah River

Warm Springs

Columbus

Andersonville

Savannah

Okefenokee Swamp

PICTURE THIS

Georgia was a great Confederate Civil War state. Picture the shape of Georgia looking like a cannon with the firing lever or lanyard on the southeast (right side) of the state. If you could pull the lanyard, a cannonball would be shot out of the top of the state.

THE CURIOUS W's

Who? My mother and father were both Baptist ministers, and I followed in their footsteps and became one, too. I was awarded the Nobel Peace Prize, and the words on my tombstone in Atlanta are "Free at last, free at last, thank God Almighty, I'm free at last." Who am I?
(answer: Martin Luther King, Jr.)

What? Three Confederate Civil War heroes, Generals Robert E. Lee, Jefferson Davis, and Stonewall Jackson tower 825 feet above the surrounding land, all on horseback. They are carved out of a gigantic granite stone mass that is the largest of its kind in the world. What is this magnificent carving?
(answer: Stone Mountain, near Atlanta)

Where? Okefenokee is fun to say, but to the early Indians it meant "Land of the Trembling Earth." Moss-draped cypress trees and wildlife of many varieties are at home in this fresh water swamp. Watch out for gators! Can you find the Okefenokee Swamp on the map? A bit of the swamp extends into Florida.

Why? The white cottage is in Warm Springs, and it was here that an American president died. He had the house built after he got polio, because he liked to bathe in the nearby mineral springs. Why is this resort famous in American history?
(answer: Known as the "Little White House," it was the favorite retreat of President Franklin D. Roosevelt.)

Make a movie in your mind. For this adventure film, picture a deep gorge between two mountains. Suddenly, the *Atlantic* Ocean rushes into the *gorge*. Gorge = Georgia, and the Atlantic = Atlanta. Atlanta is the capital of Georgia. Atlanta, Georgia!

Simply Scrumptious Easy Peach Cobbler

Here's what you need:

1 cup self-rising flour

1 cup milk

1 cup sugar

1 stick butter or margarine

about 5 large peaches, peeled and sliced.

Here's what you do: Using a mixer, cream butter and sugar until smooth. Add flour and milk alternately until well-blended. Arrange peaches in bottom of 9" cake pan, so that they're about 1½" deep. Sprinkle some brown sugar on top, if peaches are tart. Pour batter over peaches and bake at 375° for 45 minutes or until golden brown on top and cake tests done with a toothpick. Serve warm with vanilla ice cream or whipping cream. It's simply scrumptious. Thanks, Georgia!

PACK YOUR BAGS The great American Scream Machine and the Mind Bender are not for sissies. These thriller-diller roller coasters are at Six Flags Over Georgia theme park, just west of Atlanta. For a glimpse of spectacular vistas, the celebrated 2,100 mile Appalachian Trail begins in Fannin County. You can start your trek in several Georgia spots, but remember, it's a long, long hike. The trail ends in Maine!

WHO SAID THAT? The young athlete from Cairo, Georgia played four sports at UCLA, but his greatest fame came in baseball. Jack Roosevelt "Jackie" Robinson was the first black to play major league baseball in America. He's a Hall-of-Famer, and one of the game's greatest all-time players, who played 10 wonderful years with the Brooklyn Dodgers. "I will not be satisfied until I look over at a dugout and see a black face leading the team," said Jackie Robinson. His wish came true when Frank Robinson became the first black manager in the big leagues. Three cheers for Jackie Robinson's talent and determination!

NORTH CAROLINA

Sparkling rubies, sapphires, diamonds, and emeralds have been found in North Carolina. Rubies are red, sapphires are blue, diamonds can be found in all colors. Emeralds, the state gem stone, are green. Can you find an emerald-colored crayon to color North Carolina on your America! map? Or, how about the color of one of its other precious gems? You decide.

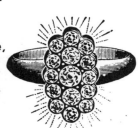

An historical anecdote tells of colonial patriots dumping barrels of tar into a stream that the Redcoats were planning to cross during the Revolutionary War. The Americans hoped that the tar would stop the British, literally, in their tracks. It worked, and from then on, or so the story goes, anyone walking in North Carolina streams got "tar heels." Along with the tar, this nickname stuck, and thus we have the Tar Heel State.

Linville

Guilford County

Raleigh

Asheville

Appalachian Mts.

Charlotte

Fayetteville

Kill Devil Hills

Cape Hatteras

Wilmington

MAPTALK

Shakespeare said that "a rose by any other name would smell as sweet." Well, not this rose. A *compass rose* is really not a rose at all. It is a small drawing on a map used to show directions. Some are drawn very fancy, indeed, but they all show where North, East, South, and West are on the map...plus all the in-betweens!

THE CURIOUS W's

 Who? I saved George Washington's portrait when the British burned the White House during the War of 1812. I simply cut the canvas out of the frame, rolled it up, and took it with me! My husband, James, was our nation's fourth President at the time. Who am I?
(answer: Dolley Payne Todd Madison, born near Guilford County)

 What? The peak of this mountain looks like the face of a sleeping old man, and nestled between two of its crests is a breath-taking bridge. This spectacular swinging bridge is over a mile high above the forested gorge. What is this wondrous mountain's name?
(answer: Grandfather Mountain, near Linville)

 Where? The "Graveyard of the Atlantic" is what Cape Hatteras is called because of the treacherous Diamond Shoals and shifting sands. Jutting out 30 miles into the Atlantic Ocean across Pamlico Sound, the cape has caused many ships to splinter and sink. Can you find Cape Hatteras?

 Why? Orville and Wilbur Wright tossed a coin, and Orville won. The rest of the day became history. The weather bureau in Washington, D.C. helped the brothers select Kill Devil Hills, because it's one of the windiest places in North America. Why is this site important? Can you place history on the map?
(answer: The first self-powered airplane flight in history took place here. Orville flew the plane first.)

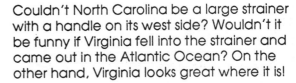

Make a movie in your mind. When you think "north" think "N" for *North* Pole and numb. Picture some Christmas *carol*ers in the cold snow. What are they doing? It's unusual, but they're lying on the cold, snowy ground shouting, *"Rah, rah, rah!"* Remember "north" goes with North Pole and numb. Carolers = Carolina. "Rah" = Raleigh. Raleigh, North Carolina. Brrr!

 ## PICTURE THIS

Couldn't North Carolina be a large strainer with a handle on its west side? Wouldn't it be funny if Virginia fell into the strainer and came out in the Atlantic Ocean? On the other hand, Virginia looks great where it is!

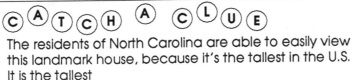

ⒸⒶⓉⒸⒽ Ⓐ ⒸⓁⓊⒺ

 The residents of North Carolina are able to easily view this landmark house, because it's the tallest in the U.S. It is the tallest
(a) television antenna
(b) lighthouse
(c) monument.
(answer: (b); clue: house = lighthouse)

NORTH CAROLINA

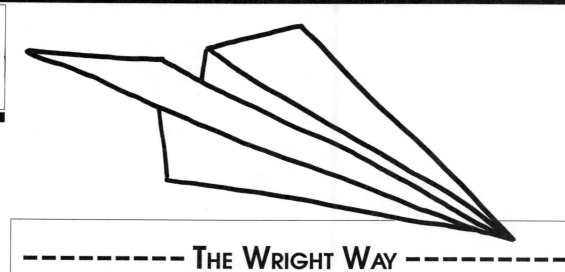

HIP, HIP, HOORAY!

A little baby girl was welcomed to the Roanoke colony when she was born to her proud parents in 1587. She was named Virginia Dare, and baby Virginia is a true American, because she was the very first English baby born in America. Happy birthday, Virginia!

HOW'S YOUR LATITUDE ATTITUDE?

Are Raleigh, North Carolina and Tokyo, Japan on the same approximate latitude (35N) as Lexington, Kentucky or Santa Fe, New Mexico?

—————— THE WRIGHT WAY ——————

The Wright brothers would definitely approve of this fun game. After all, they only used wind power at Kitty Hawk, and your planes may stay aloft longer than their first flights! *Here's what you need:* a stack of paper like used computer print-out paper or used typing paper; a hula hoop or rope, string, or yarn; a watch for timing. *Here's what you do:* Divide up into two teams and give each team a stack of paper. Someone starts timing and each team has 10 minutes to make as many paper airplanes as they can in whatever designs they want. When time is up, have two people hold the hula hoop about 8 to 10 feet back from a take-off point. (If you don't have a hula hoop, make a line to fly the planes over with the rope or string.) One team fires away. Count how many planes make it through the hoop (or over the line). Most over wins.

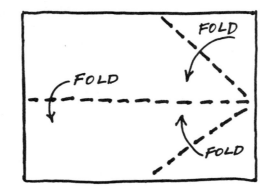

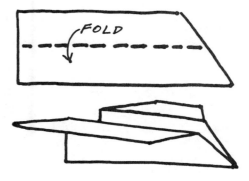

PACK YOUR BAGS

What's a wild west village doing in the Great Smokies? You can ride to the summit of the mountaintop on a chair lift or the incline railway to Ghost Town in the Sky, in Maggie Valley, but better not look down, if being elevated gives you shivers. The summit is over 3,000 feet up! Once you're there, you're in for an entertainment treat. Concerts, restaurants, and a craft village are there, but best of all is the spectacular view.

WHAT'S THE DIFFERENCE?

Climate is a pattern of weather in a certain area over many, many years. *Weather* is the state of the air and temperature at a specific place for a short time. How can you remember the difference? The *mates* in cli*mate* stay together for a long time. You *eat* every day, no matter what the w*eat*her is. Got it? Good!

·············· A HONEY OF A TREAT ···············

*T*he honeybee is North Carolina's state insect, and what do honeybees like to do best? Sting? Only if their life is threatened. What they really like to do best is make honey, and you'll love this honey treat whether you live in North Carolina or up north in Alaska.

Here's what you need:

2 cups honey
1 cup sugar
1 cup cream

Here's what you do:

1. Combine ingredients and cook slowly over very low heat until it reaches the "hard ball" or crisp state when dropped in a cupful of very cold water.

2. Have an adult help you pour the hot mixture onto a buttered cookie sheet or platter. When it is cool enough to touch, butter your hands, and "pull" back and forth, over and over, until it's a golden color and getting hard to pull.

3. Pat onto a flat plate with your hands, and cut into pieces OR roll into a long log and cut into round pieces. Any way you cut it, Honeybee Candy is Bee-licious!

South Carolina has an unusual state flower called the yellow jessamine. Wouldn't a yellow South Carolina be outstanding?

S outh Carolina is actually named for an English king, King Charles II. We usually think of Caroline as a girl's name, but in Latin, Carolina means Charles. When the original colony was divided in two, both sections kept the king's name and added North and South to their names. More Revolutionary War battles were fought here than in any other colony, and the first battle of the Civil War took place here, too. South Carolina, the *Palmetto State*, is a state of firsts that are part of America's heritage.

PACK YOUR BAGS

Wide sandy beaches make South Carolina's coast terrific for picnicking, building sand castles, and just strolling along the Atlantic shores. Swimming, boating, and fishing are summertime activities on the coast as well as on the fresh water lakes and rivers of South Carolina.

Andrew Jackson State Park

Savannah River

Columbia

Mayesville

Aiken

Georgetown

Charleston

Hilton Head

MAP TALK

We use pictures or symbols to communicate everyday — even with people who can't speak or read our language. Maps use symbols, too, and the meaning of the symbols is explained on a *map key* or *legend*. Look at a map and see how many different symbols are explained in each legend. If it's a road map, how many miles to an inch? If it's a topographical map, how can you tell where the mountains are located? How do you suppose a population map would show you how many people live in different areas? If you guessed by color, you're right. In fact, many different kinds of maps, use a *color key* to communicate lots of interesting information. Get out an atlas and take a look.

PICTURE THIS

Look closely at South Carolina and you'll see a rabbit. The northwest corner of the state is the bunny's nose. And where are its ears? They're laid flat back against his head because he is running toward the west, with his legs tucked under. Perhaps you can picture a big white fluffy tail where South Carolina, North Carolina, and the Atlantic Ocean meet. Give it a try!

THE CURIOUS W's

 Who? My parents were former slaves and I was their 17th child. I managed to get an education, even though I was a girl, and black. This was unusual for the late 1800s, but I graduated and became a teacher. I went on to start a school for black girls that is now Bethune-Cookman College. Have you ever heard my name?
(answer: It's Mary McLeod Bethune; Mayesville)

 What? This South Carolina island is one of the great recreational resorts on the Atlantic seaboard. It has tennis, golf, hiking, biking, and water sports of every kind for cooling off in the semi-tropical climate. What is this largest island on the Southeast coast?
(answer: Hilton Head)

 Where? A British officer gave me the nickname of the "Swamp Fox" because my skilled recruits and I hid on swampy islands and launched our attacks from there during the Revolutionary War. The Francis Marion National Forest was established in my memory. Can you locate this area where my soldiers and I camped while terrorizing the British?
(answer: south of Georgetown on the coast)

 Why? Cannon and mortar bombarded Fort Sumpter in Charleston Harbor for 36 hours before the garrison was allowed to leave. The band played "Yankee Doodle" and the American flag was lowered. The Confederates took control. Why is Fort Sumpter a famous fort in our history?
(answer: The first encounter of the Civil War took place here.)

 Make a movie in your mind. When you think *"south"* think "S" for sun. What is the sun shining on? It's shining on Christmas *carolers* who are standing on top of the space shuttle, *Columbia*, as it's landing. Now that would be some sight, wouldn't it? Sunny south with carolers = South Carolina. Picture the space shuttle, Columbia. Columbia = Columbia. Columbia, South Carolina.

– – – – – – Pass the Map – – – – – –

Here's what you need: 20 small pieces of paper, a map of the United States. Write North on 5 cards, South on 5, East on 5, and West on 5. *Here's what you do:* Shuffle all 20 cards. The first player calls out a state. The player to his left draws one directional card and identifies a state bordering the called state, in that direction. Example: Utah is called and south is the direction. The card holder names Arizona as a state bordering Utah on the south. Any bordering state to the south would be correct. Check the map to make sure the answer is right. Now, pass the map to the next player. Count one point for each correct answer. First person to 20 points wins.

CATCH A CLUE

 A bright red flower from Mexico was brought to the United States by Joel Poinsett, a South Carolina native. This flower has been popularized throughout the country. Its name is
(a) the Yucatan rose
(b) the Monterrey violet
(c) the poinsettia.
(answer: (c); clue: Poinsett = poinsettia)

 Get an orange and two toothpicks. Stick one toothpick in the top and one in the bottom of the orange. Pretend that these two toothpicks meet in the middle and that the orange can spin around the toothpicks, like a merry-go-round spins around its center. The imaginary toothpick pole is called an *axis*. The earth has an imaginary axis from the North Pole to the South Pole, and the earth takes one complete spin on its axis every 24 hours. Feeling dizzy?

Do dogwood trees bark? No, but they do have beautiful flowers. Virginia's state tree and flower are both the flowering dogwood. Would you like to color Virginia on your America! map a light shade of pink to look like Virginia's flowering dogwoods?

Great patriots, Revolutionary and Civil War leaders, and eight presidents have called Virginia their home. Named the "Old Dominion" by England's King Charles II, Virginia's history is also U.S. history. George Washington, Patrick Henry, Thomas Jefferson, James Madison, Robert E. Lee, Stonewall Jackson, and Booker T. Washington, were proud Virginians who became some of our first American heroes. Virginia, the *Old Dominion State* is a land of great beauty and of profound history.

PICTURE THIS

The Appalachian Mountains run from the bottom of the state to its top. Curious, isn't it, that the shape of the state of Virginia looks very much like a mountain. It is nearly straight across the base, and it rises gently to a grand peak. Do you agree?

Arlington

Westmoreland County

Blue Ridge Mountains

Richmond ✪

Williamsburg

Appomattox

Jamestown

Virginia Beach

Cumberland Gap National Park

LIGHTS, CAMERA, ACTION!

Make a movie in your mind. A very *rich man* has just asked a girl named *Virginia* for a date. And how rich is he? Well, he's so rich that he's got money pouring out of his pockets, his shoes and socks, his sleeves, and even out from under his Washington Redskins cap! (Their stadium is in Virginia.) To remember the capital of Virginia, picture that very rich man asking Virginia for a date. Rich man = Richmond, and Virginia = Virginia. Richmond, Virginia!

THE CURIOUS W's

Who? I rode my trusted horse, Traveller, on April 9, 1865, when I surrendered to General Ulysses S. Grant at the McLean House at Appomattox. I was the commanding general of the Confederate Army. Who am I?
(answer: Robert E. Lee, born in Westmoreland County)

What? This five-sided structure is the largest office building in the world. Over 25,000 people work here, mainly for the U.S. Department of Defense. The building has over 5 million square feet, which is three times that of the Empire State Building. What am I?
(answer: The Pentagon; Arlington)

Where? From a distance the ridges of these mountains look like shades of blue. This is because of the dense forests along the mountainsides. Skyline Drive is the name of the scenic highway which winds through this beautiful range of the Appalachians. Can you find the Blue Ridge Mountains?

Why? Indian Princess, Pocahontas, and her father, Chief Powhatan, lived in the area where the three ships from England anchored. The location was a little peninsula in the James River and the 100 colonists named their settlement Jamestown. Do you know why this was an important event in our history?
(answer: It was the first permanent English settlement in America.)

CATCH A CLUE

Thomas Jefferson, an accomplished musician, could make his violin sing like a bird. He also had an unusual pet to keep him company.
(a) a deer
(b) a mockingbird
(c) a raccoon
(answer: (b); clue: bird = mockingbird)

VIRGINIA

CATCH A CLUE

James Madison was no small man in American history. He is considered to be the "Father of the Constitution." He also holds another distinction.

(a) He had more formal education than any other President.
(b) He weighed the least and was the smallest of all U.S. Presidents.
(c) His picture is on the United States seal.

(answer: (b); clue: small = smallest)

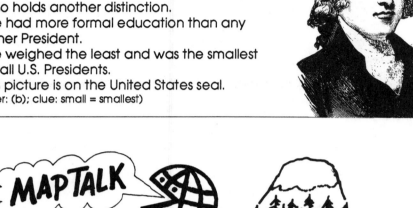

HIP, HIP, HOORAY!

"First in war, first in peace, and first in the hearts of his countrymen" is George Washington's famous epitaph. It was written by a great Revolutionary War commander, Henry "Light Horse Harry" Lee. The British gave Lee this nickname because of his lightning swift strikes and raids on the British. Three cheers for "Light Horse Harry"!

MAPTALK

Have you ever climbed a tall mountain or seen pictures of the summit (top)? There are no trees after you reach a certain altitude (height). The line where trees stop growing on a mountaintop is called the *timberline*. It is just too cold up there for them to grow.

EARTH TALK

There are two reasons why we have different seasons. The first reason is that it takes slightly more than 365 days (one year) for the earth to make one complete revolution in its orbit around the sun. The other reason is that the earth is tilted on its axis 23.5°. The tilt of the earth always stays the same. When the tilt is closest to the sun, the northern hemisphere has summer. As the earth rotates halfway around the sun, then the tilt is away from the sun and the southern hemisphere receives more direct sun rays. So when the people in the northern hemisphere are having summer, the people in the southern hemisphere are having winter, and vice versa. Brrr! Let's go for a swim!!

DID YOU KNOW ?

"Give me liberty or give me death!" gave Virginians the courage to join the rest of the colonies in the fight for independence. Who said that? It was Patrick Henry, who was governor of Virginia four times. He was also a famous orator, and his stirring speech urged Virginians to help defend the colonies against the British.

PACK YOUR BAGS

Virginia has many historical places that you won't want to miss including Arlington National Cemetery with the Tomb of the Unknown Soldier. Don't miss the changing of the guard. There's also Mount Vernon and Monticello. How about strolling around restored Williamsburg to see how people lived in days of old. Of course, for a just plain good time, don't miss Virginia Beach, an oceanside resort with boardwalks, amusement parks such as Mount Trashmore, and be sure to visit the amusement park at Busch Gardens, too. Virginia is packed with history and good times!

FEED THE BIRDS!

Virginia's many feathered creatures sometimes have a difficult time during the cold winter months. Some birds, such as Virginia's state bird, the cardinal, are ground feeders. They like their meals on the ground, and are always happy when you sprinkle seed, bread crumbs, and other special treats on the ground. Many birds like to feed from tree branches. Here's a special gourmet bird treat that they will like at any time of year!

Here's what you need:
peanut butter
a good-sized pine cone
ribbon or yarn
bird seed.

Here's what you do:

1. Tie a ribbon or piece of yarn securely in the end of the pine cone.

2. Spread peanut butter all over the pine cone, getting it into all the little nooks and crannies.

3. Pour bird seed into a pan, and roll the pine cone in the seed, covering thickly. Pat some seeds on any bare spots.

4. Hang in a tree, toward the end of a limb, and not too close to the ground. Be ready to make another one. When the birds tell their friends about this treat, there's no telling how many will show up.

Are Richmond, Virginia and Seville, Spain on the same approximate latitude (37°N) as Portland, Maine or Fargo, North Dakota?

West Virginia is every bit the *Mountain State* its nickname says. It is our only state located entirely in Appalachia. There are many small villages and towns tucked away in those beautiful hills and mountains. West Virginians are patriotic and proud. They have an outstanding voting record in national elections, and they've served our country in war and peace.

PICTURE THIS

Could that be a frog jumping out of the Ohio River? West Virginia looks like one of those little green creatures leaping out of the banks of a river. His hind legs are pushing off from Maryland and Pennsylvania. He'll be sorry if he leaves this beautiful location!

Scarlet, crimson, cardinal, and vermillion are all different names for red. Can you pick which one is also the name of West Virginia's state bird? If you picked cardinal, you know your birds! Why not color West Virginia cardinal red on your America! map.

DID YOU KNOW?

The term Appalachia is heard, read, and talked about, but where and what is Appalachia? It is the area between the Allegheny Plateau and the Allegheny Highland in the Appalachian Mountains. Can you locate Appalachia on the map?

What's in a name?

"Look, there is Jackson, standing like a stone wall. Rally behind the Virginians!" is what Bernard E. Bee said. He was looking at the daring Thomas J. Jackson on horseback, determined and ready with his men to charge in the first battle of Bull Run. From that moment on, Thomas J. Jackson became "Stonewall" Jackson, the great Confederate soldier and general of the Civil War.

Harpers Ferry

Blackwater Falls State Park

Appalachian Mts.

Point Pleasant

Charleston

Hillsboro

Lewisburg

THE CURIOUS W's

Who? When I was a baby my missionary parents took me to China, and I lived there for many years. I am a writer, and my most popular book is *The Good Earth*. I received the Pulitzer Prize for this, but I also wrote several other books. Perhaps you'll read one some-day. Do you know my name?
(answer: Pearl S. Buck; Hillsboro)

What? This U.S. armory and arsenal became very well-known when John Brown and 22 others stormed the site to steal arms and ammunition. At another time, Stonewall Jackson and his Confederate troops captured the fort and took over 12,000 Union soldiers as prisoners. What's the name of this historical landmark?
(answer: Harpers Ferry)

Where? An amazing 500 caves have been found in West Virginia, and there are hundreds more still to be explored. *Lost World* is a spectacular underground display of colorful rock formations with an ancient beach, and an enormous hall where Confederate troops attended church services underground. See if you can find Lewisburg on the map, so you'll know where this limestone wonder is.

Why? Chief Cornstalk led an Indian attack against the settlers at Point Pleasant, but the Indians were defeated. It's a very curious thing that this battle of 1774 was declared to be a first by the U.S. Senate. Why could it possibly be an important historical event?
(answer: It was declared to be the first actual battle of the Revolutionary War.)

Make a movie in your mind. Ask your mom and dad or grandparents if they know how to do the *Charleston*. Charleston is the capital of West Virginia, and if you can picture a girl named *Virginia*, who just happens to be wearing a *vest*, doing this spirited dance, you'll remember West Virginia. Charleston = Charleston. West Virginia = vest + Virginia. Charleston, West Virginia. Yeah!

STATE DRAW

Here's what you need: pencil, sheets of paper, old magazine, color America! map.
Here's what you do: When it's your turn, choose a state to draw, write it down on a piece of paper, but don't tell anyone which state it is. Put a piece of paper on a magazine, and then lie down and place the magazine and paper on your chest. The object of the game is to draw the outline of the state without look-ing at your paper and pencil. Someone can hold up the America! map for you to look at, but don't look at the paper you are drawing on. Other players guess the state you are drawing. If they guess right (only 5 guesses allowed), the artist gets 2 points, the guesser gets 1 point. Then on to the next artist. Highest scorer wins.

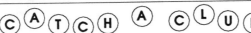
C A T C H A C L U E

It first happened in a Methodist Church in West Virginia in 1908. Mothers of America will appreciate this event.
(a) Suffrage Act of 1908
(b) the first Mothers' Day
(c) first day-care center opened
(answer: (b); clue: Mothers = Mothers')

PACK YOUR BAGS

Snow skiing in the winter and water skiing in the summer are two popular West Virginia activities. White water canoeing and rafting on the Shenan-doah and Tygart rivers makes for some of the most scenic in the country. The national kayak championships are held in Petersburg on the south branch of the Potomac River, because of the daring and challenging 15-mile white water course. West Virginia is a land-locked state, but there's plenty of water for everyone.

THE SOUTH CENTRAL STATES

N A M E   T H E   C A P I T A L

How many capitals of the South Central states can you name? Write the names below, then check your answers on the state maps. Each state capital is marked with a ✪. Did you get all seven state capitals correct?

ALABAMA _____

ARKANSAS _____

LOUISIANA _____

MISSISSIPPI _____

OKLAHOMA _____

TENNESSEE _____

TEXAS _____

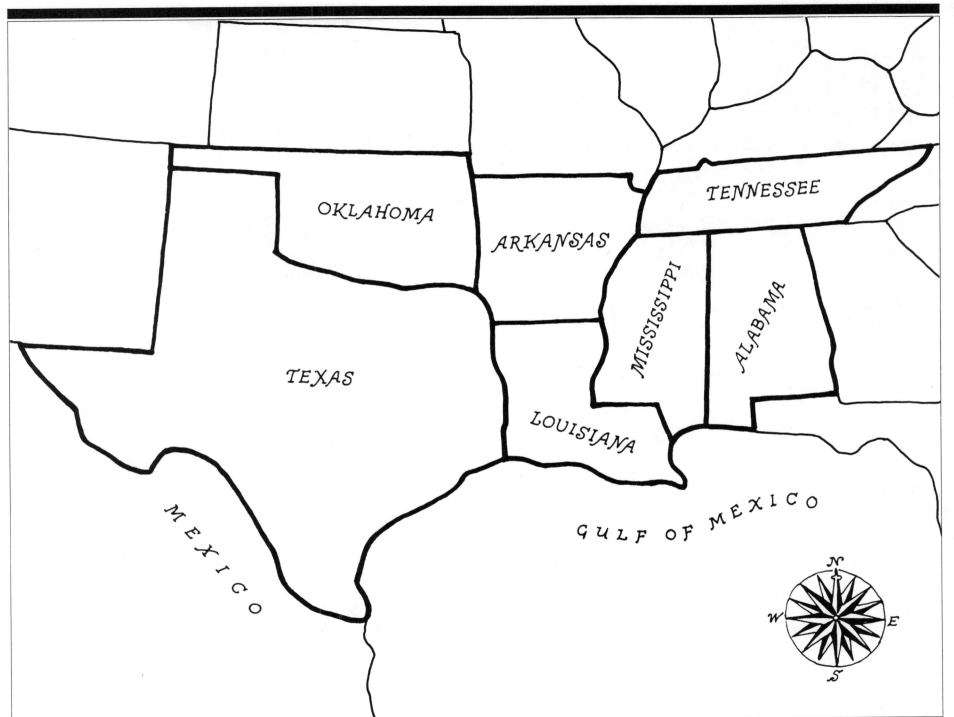

C O L O R   A M E R I C A !

Hematite is a rock of red-colored iron ore. Iron ore is used to make steel in the many foundries in Birmingham. You can visit the Red Mountain Museum and see where great chunks of the red rock are taken from a mountain. Or, you can color Alabama the color of hematite on your America! map and just pretend that you've been there.

(O)n Alabama's spectacular waterways, it is possible to ship things by barge to nearly every corner of the *Yellowhammer State*. The yellowhammer is a small yellow-feathered bird that can be seen flitting among the Southern pines, which are the state trees. This state, where cotton was once "king" on its vast plantations, has a prehistoric past, southern traditions, and the charm of the deep south.

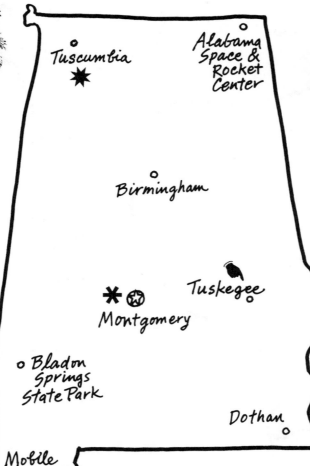

White sandy beaches on the Gulf make surf and sun the fun things to enjoy during lazy summer months. Camping is a state favorite in Alabama's beautiful, wooded state parks. What would you like to do if you visited or lived in Alabama?

MAPTALK

Do, Re, Mi. . . ooops, wrong scale. I weigh 95 pounds. . . . wrong scale again! What scale are we talking about? A *map scale*. What does it tell us? It tells distances on a map. For example, a map scale might say one inch = 20 miles. This means that for each inch on the map, it equals 20 miles. Find a map of your home state and locate the map scale. See if you can figure the distances between places in your own state. Why not try to draw a map of your town (school, library, post office, grocery store) to scale — perhaps one inch to five miles.

PICTURE THIS

Did you remember that the shape of Georgia is like a fat cannon pointing to the north with the lanyard on the lower right-hand side? Good, because Alabama also looks like a fat cannon pointing north. The only difference is that the lanyard, or firing lever, is on the left-hand side.

THE CURIOUS W's

 Who? I was only a baby when I lost all sight and hearing. When I was seven years old, Anne Sullivan came to live with my family. She taught me to read by braille, and she spelled out words on my hand with her fingers. This allowed me to communicate for the very first time in my life. I graduated from college and wrote many books. Who am I?
(answer: Helen Keller, Tuscumbia)

 What? Booker T. Washington founded this Alabama college for black students who wanted a higher education. George Washington Carver was one of the instructors. Do you know the name of this school?
(answer: Tuskegee Institute in Tuskegee)

 Where? The first White House of the Confederacy is located here. It was the home of Jefferson Davis and the capital of the southern states. Now it is the capital of Alabama. Can you find Montgomery on the map?

 Make a movie in your mind. Can you imagine filming an enormous *mount*ain of *gum* — bubble gum, spearmint gum, cinnamon gum, all kinds of gum? And just what is that sitting on top of the mountain of gum? An *owl!* Think of an owl to remember Alabama. Mount + gum = Montgomery. Owl = Alabama. Montgomery, Alabama. You won't forget.

JUST IMAGINE

Your legs and arms feel like feathers as they start to slowly rise. You seem to float on air without any support beneath your body. Are you hovering above the earth in a space shuttle? Are you attached to a lifeline attempting a spacewalk? You're still on earth, but you're on a zero-G machine that makes you think you're a million miles away. The Alabama Space and Rocket Center lets you pretend to be an astronaut for a few hours. Try guiding a spacecraft by computer or feel the blast of rocket engines during liftoff. Just imagine what it would be like to be an astronaut.

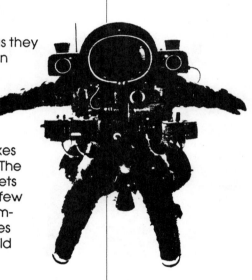

CATCH A CLUE

 A wise Confederate citizen is remembered for his historic ride from Gadsden, Alabama to Rome, Georgia to warn the people that the Union Army was approaching. This southern Paul Revere was
(a) Joe Samuelson
(b) John Wisdom
(c) Jefferson Davis.
(answer: (b); clue: wise = Wisdom)

SHAKE A STATE

Write each state's name on a small piece of paper. Put all 50 pieces of paper into a brown paper bag. Shake the bag and each player draws one state at a time, identifying the capital of the state he draws. If the answer is correct, you keep the state name. If incorrect, put it back in the bag. Player with the most states at the end wins.

ARKANSAS

Is a tomato a fruit or a vegetable? The people in Arkansas know, because the state *fruit* is the South Arkansas vine-ripened pink tomato! If you color Arkansas pink on your America! map, there won't be another state colored for a pink tomato!

Arkansas, the *Natural State*, used to be nicknamed the Bear State for good reason. The Ozarks were filled with black bears! No wonder Davy Crockett became a folk hero. People born in Arkansas tend to stay there, and they love passing along folklore about animals, people, and events. Another state favorite are the Razorbacks, named by a University of Arkansas football coach, way back in 1909, who said his team resembled "a wild bunch of razorback hogs."

o Fayetteville

∧ ∧ ∧
∧   ∧
∧ Ozark Mts.
∧   ∧ ∧

Blytheville o

Ozark National Forest

Arkansas River

Little Rock ⊛

Helena o

Hot Springs National Park

✳ o Murfreesboro

o Texarkana
"

Stalactites and stalagmites are calcium carbonate deposits found in caves. *Stalactites* are formed on the roof of the cave, and they look like icicles hanging down. *Stalagmites* are formed on the floor of the cave from dripping water, and they look like they're growing from the floor up. There's an easy way to remember which is which. Stalac*tites* have to hang on *tight* so they won't fall off the ceiling. Doesn't this help you remember the difference?

DID YOU KNOW?

PICTURE THIS

Look at the state of Arkansas and you'll see that two opposite corners have notches taken out of them. The northeast (top right) corner and the southwest (bottom left) corner have chunks missing. This is our only state with this unusual feature which makes it easy to remember.

HOW'S YOUR LATITUDE ATTITUDE?

Are Little Rock, Arkansas and Algeria, Africa on the same approximate latitude (34°N) as Huntsville, Alabama or Las Vegas, Nevada?

THE CURIOUS W's

Who? "I shall return," is what I promised the people of the Philippines after President Franklin D. Roosevelt ordered me to leave. I was then given the command of the Allied forces in the southwest Pacific. I'm also the Army general who accepted Japan's surrender which ended World War II. Who am I?
(answer: Douglas MacArthur, born in Little Rock)

What? Hernando de Soto probably discovered the 47 natural hot springs over 400 years ago. Today, the site is a national park. What is the name of this Arkansas national park?
(answer: Hot Springs National Park)

Where? A tourist found a huge diamond, over 16-carats in size, in the only diamond field in North America. Tourists can still dig for diamonds at Crater of Diamonds State Park which is one of America's true natural wonders. This one-of-a-kind site is near Murfreesboro.

Why? The name of the city is Texarkana, and it's located in the southwest corner of the state. There really are two Texarkanas, two city governments, two sets of city services, but only one post office. Why?
(answer: Texarkana is built on the Arkansas-Texas border, so there's a Texarkana, Arkansas, and a Texarkana, Texas. They share the same post office.)

LIGHTS, CAMERA, ACTION!

Make a movie in your mind. There's something out there in the water! What is it? Why, it's an ark with animals on it. But there's something else going on. Millions of *little rocks* are falling from the sky on top of the ark as the animals run below deck. When you think of Arkansas, think of the ark. The capital city is Little Rock. Ark = Arkansas, and little rocks = Little Rock. Little Rock, Arkansas.

PACK YOUR BAGS

If you dig rocks, you'll love digging for your own quartz crystals in Coleman's Crystal Mine. It's north of Hot Springs, and while you're in the area, stop at the Mid-America Museum for some fun, hands-on experiments. The Magic Springs Family Attraction theme park is also just minutes away. North Central Arkansas is home to the state's well-known crafts-people and music-makers, and the Ozark Folk Center in Mountain View showcases the homemade crafts and music of the Ozarks. There's plenty to do in Arkansas!

WHO SAID THAT?

General Douglas MacArthur, after being relieved from his Far East command, uttered these famous words while addressing Congress: "Old soldiers never die; they just fade away."

CATCH A CLUE

A picture of this mountain has never appeared on the cover of *Life* or *Time*, but it's the tallest mountain in Arkansas, rising to a height of 2,753 feet. The name of this mountain is
(a) Mount Bear
(b) Mount Razorback
(c) Mount Magazine.
(answer: (c); clue: *Life, Time* = Magazine)

SAW OR SASS?

If Kansas is pronounced can-sass, then how come Arkansas isn't pronounced ar-can-sass? Good question, but the fact is that Arkansas is pronounced ar-can-saw, and that's the way it is folks!

Bayou, Cajun, Creole, Dixieland jazz, Bourbon Street, and gumbo are words that come to mind when we think of Louisiana. The mighty Mississippi River and the Gulf of Mexico have helped shape the state's history and customs. Great forests of pines and swamps of cypress add to Louisiana's colorful vistas, and the subtropical climate nourishes lush vegetation from Spanish moss to brilliant pink azaleas that grow wild. Louisiana's varied cultures and natural beauty are boundless.

If you've ever sung "You Are My Sunshine" then you already know one of Louisiana's state songs. What a perfect color for your America! map, the color of sunshine. Louisiana gets lots of rain, too, but when sun shines down on the *Pelican State*, Louisiana's alligators and sea turtles probably feel like singing too! How about a bright yellow-orange for Louisiana sunshine?

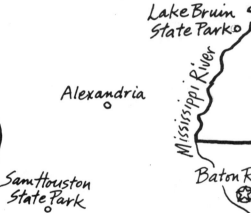

o Shreveport

Lake Bruin State Park o

Mississippi River

Alexandria

Sam Houston State Park

Baton Rouge ✪

Lake Pontchartrain

New Orleans

*

PICTURE THIS

Have you seen pictures of the old-time steam engines with the tall smokestacks? Louisiana is shaped like one of these "iron horses" from the past. See the smokestack? The engine is heading west. All aboard!

PACK YOUR BAGS

Famous for its festivals, Louisianans love to celebrate with food, dancing parades, parties, and carnivals. They even have a festival honoring sweet potatoes! Does your state have any unusual festivals?

DID YOU KNoW ?

Lake Pontchartrain is a *brackish* lake. Brackish means that the lake is a mixture of fresh water and salt water. Can you see on the map why the two waters mix?

THE CURIOUS W's

 What? Fat Tuesday is the literal English translation for this world-famous festival. Street parades, balls, floats, parties, and feasts highlight the festivities. Everyone in the gala parade wears a mask except the king, who is called Rex. Do you know what this grand New Orleans' French tradition is called?
(answer: Mardi Gras, New Orleans)

 Where? "Great River" is what the native Americans called this massive waterway. Hernando de Soto was probably the first white man to see the river, and when he died, it became his final resting place. "Old Man River" is how those on its shores affectionately refer to the river. Can you find where the Mississippi empties into the Gulf of Mexico?
(answer: just below New Orleans)

 Why? It's 24 miles long and it's built over Lake Pontchartrain in southern Louisiana. The Lake Pontchartrain Causeway opened in 1956, but it still holds a world record. Can you guess why?
(answer: It's the longest bridge in the world.)

 **LIGHTS, CAMERA, ACTION!**

A sports-minded girl named *Louise* is stepping up to the plate at a crucial moment in a softball game. All eyes are on Louise. What is she doing? To the shock of the crowd, she takes the *bat* and uses it to put *rouge* on her cheeks! *Louise* = Louisiana, and bat + rouge = Baton Rouge. Baton Rouge, Louisiana!

ALL THAT JAZZ!

It can be hot, cool, or sweet, but it has nothing to do with potatoes. It's jazz! It started as a blend of black and Creole music in New Orleans around the turn of the century. Some say it's a combination of just about every rhythm, beat, tempo, and harmony imaginable. It was originally played at black funerals, and it can be blues or gospel, folk or classical. Whatever it is, we know it's American and our gifted musicians like Louis "Satchmo" Armstrong, Earl Hines, and Duke Ellington made the whole world swing to the beat.

LOUISIANA LINGO

Bayou: A bayou is a slow-moving waterway which is an inlet or outlet of a river, lake, or even the ocean. Most of Louisiana's bayous used to be mouths of the Mississippi River.

Cajun: Louisianans who are descendants of the Acadians (French settlers of an area in eastern Canada) are called Cajuns. After being driven out by the British, the Acadians slowly made their way to Louisiana, where they finally settled.

Creole: This term describes descendants of early French or Spanish settlers in the Gulf states. Today, the term also refers to the particular culture these descendants have preserved.

Gumbo: A gumbo is a Cajun favorite stew made with fish or meat, okra, peppers, and onions. It is served over rice.

Jambalaya: This rich rice and seafood chowder is a famous Louisiana meal. If you visit, be sure to try it.

HIP, HIP, HOORAY!

James John Audubon did 435 paintings of over 1000 birds. He painted these life-like masterpieces in New Orleans over a period of 12 years. His Birds of America is considered to be one of the greatest collections of prints ever produced. Isn't it curious that he had to travel to London to find an engraver to reproduce his work because no one in America thought they would sell? Audubon was a great naturalist and conservationist . . . and artist!

COLOR AMERICA!

The Magnolia State is named for the state tree and flower, the magnolia. Its large, thick petals are white and fragrant. Can you think of some other plant that is white, that used to be the most important crop in Mississippi? It's cotton. The white of magnolias and cotton could look very impressive on your America! map.

The influence of Native Americans, early European settlers, and the Civil War can be sensed throughout this beautiful Magnolia State. When the European explorers arrived, the Natchez, Choctaw, and Chickasaw were already there. Known for its southern hospitality and its spectacular flowering and wooded landscape, Mississippi today is a sparkling gift from its historic past.

HIP, HIP, HOORAY!

Historians tell about events, while writers tell us about people and feelings and life. A round of applause for Mississippi authors who have given the world a first-hand picture of plantations and slavery, the common folk and the rich. Names America knows are William Faulkner, Tennessee Williams, Eudora Welty, Richard Wright, and Hodding Carter.

PACK YOUR BAGS

When hundreds of shrimp boats are decorated and the Blessing of the Fleet takes place in the waters of the Gulf at Biloxi, it's a sight to behold. Festivals, fairs, music celebrations, horse shows, competitions, sports, and pilgrimages also keep people entertained every week of the year in this state where people love to participate.

PICTURE THIS

The state of Mississippi looks like a chopping knife with the blade facing west. Can you see the handle? For some reason the blade is uneven, probably because it's been chopping away at the banks of the Mississippi River. The Mississippi River is the entire western boundary of the state of Mississippi.

THE CURIOUS W's

 Who? After I had created my friends, Kermit the Frog and Miss Piggy, I knew that it was love at first sight. At the time I didn't know that these two Muppets along with Bert and Ernie, Big Bird, and the rest of the Sesame Street gang would become world-famous celebrities. Do you know who I am?
(answer: Jim Henson, Greenville)

 What? The Floating Circus Palace seated over 3,000 people as it churned its way up and down the Mississippi River. It was a floating theater that brought musicals, dramas, and other exciting entertainment to people who lived along the banks of the Great River. Many paddle-wheel boats are still in use today. Do you know what these theaters are called?
(answer: showboats; Mississippi River)

 Where? Memorial Day, on May 30, is the day Americans honor those who have died in battle defending our country. The very first Memorial Day was held after the Civil War in 1866 when several ladies from the town decorated the graves of Confederate and Union soldiers at Friendship Cemetery. Do you know where it is located?
(answer: Columbus)

 Why? Nearly 600 houses and buildings built before the Civil War are still standing in Natchez, an historic city built on a bluff above the Mississippi River where the Natchez Indians once lived. Why is Natchez so prized and cherished by its residents?
(answer: Natchez is the oldest city on the Mississippi River.)

LIGHTS, CAMERA, ACTION!

Make a movie in your mind. When you think of Mississippi do you think of the great Mississippi River? Now see the action of Tom Sawyer and Huckleberry Finn floating on a raft down the Mississippi River, playing jacks. That would be some sight. *Jacks on* the *Mississippi* = Jackson, Mississippi. Now you know another state and its capital.

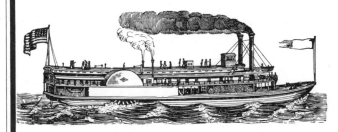

EARTH TALK

The United States is part of the North American continent. Continent means "self-contained." There are seven continents on Earth. The other continents are Asia, Africa, South America, Antarctica, Europe, and Australia. Think of a report card with six A's and one E. That will help you remember them: Asia, Africa, America (north), America (south), Antarctica, Australia, and what's the E? Europe.

DID YOU KNOW?

Mississippi still bears the battle scars from the Civil War because it endured the highest percentage of lives lost than any other state. When W.T. Sherman, the Union general, saw the terrible destruction of this beautiful state, he said, "War is hell!" Many people since have quoted the general's famous words.

CATCH A CLUE

 It leaves one amazed to know that Mississippi leads the nation in
(a) earthworm production
(b) tree farming
(c) computer manufacturing.
(answer: (b); clue: leaves = tree)

OKLAHOMA

Two Choctaw Indian words, "okla" which means people and "hummus" which means red, make up the word "Oklahoma." The Choctaw Indians might be proud if you selected their word, "hummus" for the color of Oklahoma on your America! map. Oklahoma means "home of the red man."

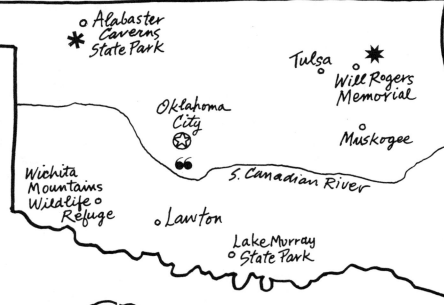

Oklahoma has binding ties to its Native American Indian and cowboy cultures. You can sense it in the names of cities and streets, taste the flavor in the food, and hear it in music and song. Oklahoma is proud of its frontier beginnings. One of the largest buffalo herds in the world is situated near Lawton, and coyotes, armadillos, and antelope are still roaming the plains. But, Oklahoma has progressive cities too, where the performing arts represent some of the best talent in the country. It's a land of mixed cultures and land regions. As the state song says, "You're doin' fine, Oklahoma! Oklahoma O.K.!"

PICTURE THIS

Oklahoma looks like a pan with the handle of the pan pointing west. This part of the state is actually called the "panhandle." Take a look and see if you can see the pan with a handle.

THE CURIOUS W's

Who? I don't know how good of an actor I was, because I never really acted. I wrote newspaper columns and books, but I'm most famous for my homespun cowboy humor and rope twirling which I performed on stage. My life ended in a plane crash in Alaska. Who am I?
(answer: Will Rogers; born in Oologah, Indian Territory; now Oklahoma)

What? Sequoya was born in Tennessee, but when the Indians were removed from their homelands, he came to Oklahoma. His mother was Cherokee and his father was Caucasian. He lived with the Cherokees and spent 12 years developing an amazing system of characters. What did Sequoya invent?
(answer: a Cherokee alphabet that was used to publish newspapers and books in their own language; lived near Sallislaw)

Where? Hues of multicolored crystals and alabaster can be seen in the wonderful formations in Alabaster Caverns State Park. This exceptional display of gypsum makes it the largest public gypsum cave in America. Nearby is a canyon with a natural rock bridge spanning the gap. Where are these caverns?
(answer: about 30 miles north of Woodward in the northwest part of the state)

Why? At noon on April 22, 1889, two million acres of land previously leased to the Indians went up for grabs. An official fired a pistol and the Land Run of 1889 began. Why was this important to what is now the state of Oklahoma?
(answer: Fifty thousand people rushed to Oklahoma seeking land. Oklahoma City was founded in one day by over 10,000 people who staked claim to that site.)

Ⓒ Ⓐ Ⓣ Ⓒ Ⓗ Ⓐ Ⓒ Ⓛ Ⓤ Ⓔ

In the wild areas of Oklahoma, oil was discovered. Oil prospectors drilled early wells, and these oil prospectors were known as
(a) fossil fuel engineers
(b) black gold explorers
(c) wildcatters.
(answer: (c); clue: wild = wild)

LIGHTS, CAMERA, ACTION!

Make a movie in your mind. Picture two large oak trees growing out of your home. In one of the oak trees is a little kitty. Can you hear it meow? *Oak in your home* = Oklahoma. *Oak in your home with the kitty* = Oklahoma City. Oak + home = Oklahoma. Oak + home + kitty = Oklahoma City. Oklahoma City, Oklahoma.

Some Sooners Got There Later

Some of the eager land seekers didn't want to wait for the appointed date to cross into Oklahoma Territory and stake a land claim. So, what did these greedy settlers do? They cheated! They sneaked into the territory ahead of time. Some of them even tried to fool the officials by running their horses and wagons hard so that it looked like they had just arrived. These too anxious folks were labeled as "Sooners," and the name stuck. Many got caught and ended up having to go to the end of the line at the border. Today, Oklahoma residents are known as *Sooners*, the state's nickname.

OKLAHOMA

JUST IMAGINE

During the winter of 1838 -1839 Cherokee and other Indian tribes were forced to leave their homes in the southern Appalachian Mountains and move to the Indian Territory which is now called Oklahoma. What would it be like to see your belongings stolen or destroyed and your home burned to the ground? Over 4,000 Cherokees were buried along the route that became known as the "Trail of Tears." They died from exposure to the severe cold, from disease, and starvation. The "Trail of Tears" was a sad event in America's history.

WHO SAID THAT?

"All I know is what I read in the papers," is how humorist Will Rogers began his stage performances. He would then go on to make people laugh by poking fun at presidents, royalty, and prominent people of the day. He frequently said that he'd never met a man he didn't like, and everyone liked Will Rogers.

HIP, HIP, HOORAY!

King Gustaf V of Sweden called him "the greatest athlete in the world" after he won both the decathlon and pentathlon in the 1912 Olympic Games in Stockholm, Sweden. He was the only person to ever accomplish such an amazing athletic feat. He was born near Prague, Oklahoma, the son of Native Americans, and he attended Carlisle Indian School in Pennsylvania, where he met Pop Warner, the great football coach, who helped Thorpe develop into a track and football star. Jim Thorpe, Native American, makes all Americans proud.

EARTH TALK

Buffalo herds roam the lone prairie, and cowboys ride across the plains. What's the difference between a *prairie* and a *plain*? Not much, except the spelling. They're both names for lowlands. The lowlands cover about 1,500 miles between the Rocky Mountains and the Appalachian Mountains.

MAKE A SOUTHWESTERN-STYLED HEADBAND

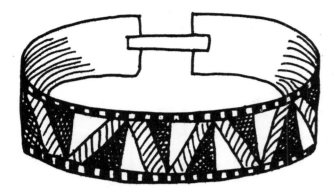

Here's a great headband you can wear to keep your hair out of your eyes while playing sports, or just to look great! They are perfect for boys and girls alike.

Here's what you need:

> **A felt strip, about 1" x 16"**
>
> **Assorted colorful felt scraps**
>
> **Sequins, buttons, and other trims**
>
> **3/4" elastic, about 4" long**
>
> **White glue**
>
> **Needle and thread**

Here's what you do:

1. Cut the felt scraps into various shapes - either a design or symbols or whatever suits your mood. Glue them to one side of the long felt strip, using the glue sparingly.

2. Add other trims, if you like.

3. Sew the elastic to the inside of the headband at both ends. Now, wear with pride.

(ADAPTED FROM *ADVENTURES IN ART* BY SUSAN MILORD)

There were five Indian tribes in the southeastern part of the United States that became known as the Five Civilized Tribes. They were given this name because they began accepting the lifestyle and customs of the Europeans and Caucasian Americans. These tribes were the Cherokee, the Choctaw, the Creek, the Seminole, and the Chickasaw. Curious, isn't it, that we saw as civilized only those who accepted our ways. What do you think about that now?

A – O.K., Oklahomans!

Mickey Mantle, Warren Spahn, and Johnny Bench batted, pitched, and caught their way into baseball's record books. These three favorite sons are known to Little Leaguers and baseball fans of all ages. Olympic gold-medal winner Bart Connor and world champion wrestler, John Smith, have also helped put Oklahoma on America's sports' map.

PACK YOUR BAGS

Rodeos and other horse-related activities top the list of things to do and see in Oklahoma. Rodeo championships, horse shows, polo matches, and horse racing are for the serious minded, but horseback riding and guided trail rides can be enjoyed by anyone. Indian powwows are held throughout the state, and if you like contests, there are some real winners. How about the Shortgrass Rattlesnake Derby in Mangum, the Walleye (fish) Rodeo in Canton, the Rooster Day Celebration in Broken Arrow, or the Brick and Rolling Pin Throwing Contest in Stroud? And if those aren't enough, you can always sharpen up for the Cow Chip Throwing Contest in Beaver!

C O L O R   A M E R I C A !

Tennessee's state flower is the iris which blooms in white, and shades of yellow and purple. Purple is the most usual color. You probably have just the right purple or lavender for the state that has "Tennessee: America at its best!" as its state motto. Do you?

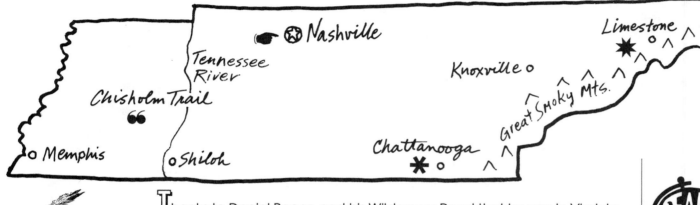

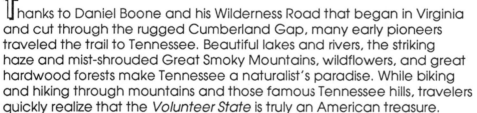

Thanks to Daniel Boone and his Wilderness Road that began in Virginia and cut through the rugged Cumberland Gap, many early pioneers traveled the trail to Tennessee. Beautiful lakes and rivers, the striking haze and mist-shrouded Great Smoky Mountains, wildflowers, and great hardwood forests make Tennessee a naturalist's paradise. While biking and hiking through mountains and those famous Tennessee hills, travelers quickly realize that the *Volunteer State* is truly an American treasure.

PICTURE THIS

Do you know that an anvil is used for shaping horseshoes? Look at the state of Tennessee, and you'll see that it looks like an anvil. The state horse is the Tennessee walking horse, and that will help you remember that anvils are used to make horseshoes for the walking horse.

EARTH TALK

A mountain is a landform that's usually over 1,000 feet high. What is the tallest mountain in your state? Can you name two famous mountain ranges, one in the western U.S. and one in the eastern part of the nation? Of course you can — the Rocky Mountains in the West and Appalachians in the East.

HOW'S YOUR LATITUDE ATTITUDE? 😊

Are Nashville, Tennessee and Tunis, Tunisia on the same approximate latitude (36°N) as Tulsa, Oklahoma or Phoenix, Arizona?

THE CURIOUS W's

 Who? Not all the songs and stories about me are true, but I did kill 105 bears in nine months. I was a hunter, scout, frontiersman, soldier, and a congressman. I'm identified in folklore by my coonskin hat. I was killed defending the Alamo in San Antonio, Texas. Who am I?
(answer: David "Davy" Crockett; probably near Limestone in eastern Tennessee)

 What? Andrew Jackson built this white mansion in 1819 for his wife, Rachel, who died less than a month before her husband was inaugurated as President. Fire destroyed much of the home at one time, but it was rebuilt, and Jackson retired here. What is the name of this historic home?
(answer: The Hermitage, Nashville)

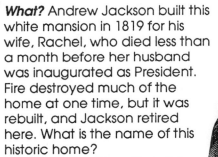

Where? "Chat-to-to-noog-gee" is what the Creek Indians called Lookout Mountain. It means "rock rising to a point." From its top, it is said that you can see seven states on a clear day. Beneath the mountain are underground caverns and waterfalls. Find Chattanooga, and see if you can locate Lookout Mountain.

Why? Jesse Chisholm was a Cherokee Indian who drove a wagon west across the indian territory that is now Oklahoma. He opened trading posts in Kansas and Oklahoma. Cattle drivers followed his wagon ruts to Abilene, Kansas, and the Texas cattlemen driving their herds made the trip famous. Why?
(answer: It was the beginning of the Chisholm Trail, famous for its cattle drives.)

 During the Mexican War, there were 30,000 volunteers from the state of Tennessee. The government only called for 2,800 volunteers. No wonder Tennessee is The *Volunteer State!*

 Make a movie in your mind. Picture a *tennis* player *smashing* a large *pill* over the net, instead of a ball. Smash + pill = Nashville, and tennis = Tennessee. Nashville, Tennessee.

STARS & STRIPES GAME

Hurray for the red, white, and blue! Identify things that are colored red, white, or blue (example: red fire engine) or have red, white, or blue in their name (example: blueberries). The object of the game is to see who can think of the most reds, whites, and blues, until only one player is left. Only four seconds to think or you are out. The color of the objects must be in sequence — first person names a red object, second player a white, third names a blue, next names a red, again. Last one still in the game, wins.

He learned to shoot a rifle as a small boy growing up in the mountains of Tennessee. This experience helped him during World War I, when he and seven other soldiers, upon discovering a German machine gun nest, captured 132 Germans and killed 25 others. He was only a corporal then, but he became known as Sergeant York. His name is Alvin Cullum York, from Pall Mall, Tennessee and all America loved this war hero who said that he never wanted to go to war. He just felt that it was his duty to serve his country.

TEXAS

The *Lone Star State*, neighbor to Mexico, and until 1959, the biggest state in the Union, has something of everything. There are deserts, flatlands that stretch for miles, mountains, islands, forests, jungles, marshy bayous, ranches, farmlands, and ocean beaches along the Gulf. Texas has oil and other natural resources, and it also has hurricanes. Texas still has small towns with their old west flavor, but it also has its big cities where business, industry, and culture flourish.

It isn't the state song, and the rose isn't the state flower, but "The Yellow Rose of Texas" is one of the most popular songs ever written about the state. If you'd like to color Texas yellow on your America! map, make sure you've got a good-sized crayon because Texas is big!

Amarillo

Red River

Fort Worth

Dallas

El Paso

Monahans Sandhill State Park

Colorado River

Austin

San Jacinto

Big Bend National Park

Rio Grande River

Houston

San Antonio

MEXICO

GULF OF MEXICO

Laredo

Corpus Cristi

PICTURE THIS

Texas is easily recognized by its unusual shape and size. Look at the southern part of the state, and see if you think it looks like the rudder of a boat. Do you agree? This is one state that most people can easily identify because of its shape and bigness. Can you?

THE CURIOUS W's

 Who? A Cherokee chief adopted me after I ran away from home when I was 13 years old. I later became the governor of Tennessee, commander of the Texas army, twice president of the Republic of Texas, and a U.S. senator. I was the general in command when Texas won its independence, by defeating the Mexican army. Who am I?
(answer: Sam Houston; born in Virginia but spent most of his life in Texas)

 What? Folk hero frontiersmen Davy Crockett, James Bowie, and William Travis with 186 other patriots fought thousands of Mexican troops for 13 days. The Americans were finally overrun by Santa Anna and his forces, and the brave fighters for Texas' independence were all killed. What is the name of this old mission and historic site where this famous battle took place?
(answer: The Alamo, San Antonio)

Where? "Bones of a prehistoric pterodactyl were found at this site that is located along an international border. This flying reptile with a 38-foot wing span became extinct over 60 million years ago, but one can picture these gigantic reptiles flying over the inland sea which once covered this area. Can you find Big Bend National Park?

Why? General Sam Houston and his troops defeated over twice as many Mexicans led by Santa Anna on the banks of the San Jacinto River. Do you know why this battle and brilliant victory changed history for Texas and the United States?
(answer: It was the final battle between the U.S. and Mexico that gave Texas its independence. San Jacinto)

CATCH A CLUE

Popeye would love the state of Texas because it's first in the production of
(a) pecans
(b) spinach
(c) granite.
(answer: (b); clue: Popeye = spinach)

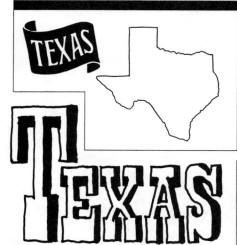

TEXAS

Everyone likes to be the best or the biggest, or the most or the longest of something or other. Texans are teased about doing everything in a big way, because, of course, they come from such a big state. But lots of people like to break records. Get a copy of *The Guiness Book of World Records* out of the library. See any records you and your friends might want to challenge, like the longest time playing ping-pong or building the biggest Lego® tower, or thinking the hardest about what record you might break.

Create A State

With family or friends, take a 15-minute walk around your neighborhood or another location. From this walk, have fun creating your own state. Make the shape of your state by the directions you walk. It could be a circular state, a square state, a zigzag state, or any other shape. Select a state bird, tree, flower, and animal from what you actually observed on your walk. Give your state a name, a motto, and a nickname. Designate the capital of your state at a location somewhere within the boundaries of your walk. You can even create a state flag. Make a map of your new state using a scale, a compass rose, symbols, roads, landmarks, and maybe even the population. Once you create your own state, perhaps you and your friends might want to create a new nation!

!!!!!!!!!!SPORTS FEVER!!!!!!!!!

Take your pick of teams to root for in Texas for your weekend's excitement. High school and college rivalries are intense, and entire towns turn out for athletic competitions. Professional teams like the Dallas Cowboys and the Houston Oilers thrill football fans each fall. The Houston Astros and the Texas Rangers play Major League baseball, and basketball fans have plenty to cheer about with the Houston Rockets and the San Antonio Spurs. Although cowboys are slowly disappearing, rodeos are still high on the popularity list, and they're held all over the state throughout the year. When you're in Texas, sports fever is contagious!

WHO SAID THAT?

When Sam Houston found out that the Mexican troops usually took a little siesta at a certain time each day, he decided that their nap time would be a good time to attack. The Mexican army was caught by surprise and defeated as the Texans charged into their camp shouting, "Remember the Alamo!"

LIGHTS, CAMERA, ACTION!

Make a movie in your mind. You're going to the dentist, and your dentist is in an unusual location. His chair is in a *taxi!* While you're sitting in the chair in the taxi, your dentist tells you to say, *"Aaah."* He then fills your teeth with *tin* (very strange). Taxi = Texas, and "aaah" + tin = Austin. The capital of Texas is Austin. Austin, Texas. You'll now have a tin grin!

Tsunami. What a funny word, tsunami; it's the Japanese name for tidal wave. Tidal waves start in the ocean after an earthquake. If it's deep under the water, the wave can travel as fast as a jet plane, but if the water is shallow, it will travel as slow as someone on a bicycle. Why is this wave important? When a tidal wave hits land, it can be as high as a 12-story building, and it can make a huge, destructive splash.

HIP, HIP, HOORAY!

This talented person was a track star, golfer, swimmer, basketball, baseball, and football player, boxed a little, and played pocket billiards. Mildred "Babe" Didrikson Zaharias from Port Arthur set records in the 80-meter hurdles and javelin throw in the 1932 Olympic Games in Los Angeles. She was an All-America woman's basketball player, and she set an amazing women's golfing record by winning 17 major tournaments in a row. What an athlete!

PACK YOUR BAGS

Have you practiced your watermelon-seed spitting lately? There's a contest for this each year at the Great Watermelon Thump held in Luling. If you're a chili lover, you won't want to miss the world famous World's Champion Chili Cook-off, in November in Terlingua, where you get to sample the entries. San Antonio has its Fiesta in April, and there's a parade with all the trimmings attended by thousands. Texans love fairs, and the Texas State Fair in Dallas is the biggest attended event in the country. Does it surprise you that Texas holds more fairs, festivals, and special events than any other state?

THE NORTH CENTRAL STATES

N A M E   T H E   C A P I T A L

How many capitals of the North Central states can you name? Write the names below, then check your answers on the state maps. Each state capital is marked with a ✪. Did you get all thirteen state capitals correct?

ILLINOIS _____

INDIANA _____

IOWA _____

KANSAS _____

KENTUCKY _____

MICHIGAN _____

MINNESOTA _____

_____ **MISSOURI**

_____ **NEBRASKA**

_____ **NORTH DAKOTA**

_____ **OHIO**

_____ **SOUTH DAKOTA**

_____ **WISCONSIN**

COLOR AMERICA!

Nearly 2,500 plants grow wild in Illinois, and the spring-time blossoms can be found on river and stream banks, in forests, and on the plains. Since the native violet is the state flower of this *Land of Lincoln*, can you find a violet color for your America! map?

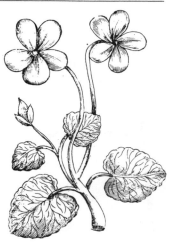

When ancient glaciers covered much of America, they did Illinois a big favor. They deposited some of the richest, thickest soil which is why the state is always a leader in the production of soybeans, corn, and other agricultural products. Many people live in the cities now, but the fertile, black soil of Illinois still produces. Chicago not only has the tallest building in the world with the Sears Tower, but it also leads all cities in manufacturing. Its location has given the city great shipping, railroads, and air traffic. Its airport is the busiest in the world. Illinois, the land of changeable weather, is one of our nation's melting pots of immigrants, which makes it a true all-American state.

Chicago

* Starved Rock State Park

La Salle

Galesburg

○ Peoria

Springfield

Lincoln Log Cabin State Park

East St. Louis

Mississippi River

HOW'S YOUR LATITUDE ATTITUDE?

Are Springfiled, Illinois and Valencia, Spain on the same approximate latitude (39°N) as Des Moines, Iowa or Denver, Colorado?

EARTH TALK

Atmosphere is the layer of air that surrounds the earth, and it's made up of several gasses, mostly nitrogen and oxygen. Take a deep breath!

PICTURE THIS

Look for the profile of a person at the top left side of the state, looking to the northwest. You can see the ridge of the eyebrow, the nose, and the mouth is open like he's blowing air in an upward direction. Can you find this? Notice that the top of the head is flat.

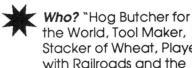

THE CURIOUS W's

Who? "Hog Butcher for the World, Tool Maker, Stacker of Wheat, Player with Railroads and the Nation's Freight Handler; Stormy, husky, brawling, City of the Broad Shoulders." This is part of a poem I wrote about Chicago. I'm also known for my biography of Abraham Lincoln. Who am I?
(answer: Carl Sandburg; Galesburg)

What? Something terrible happened in Chicago one October night in 1871. It started in Patrick O'Leary's barn, and it left Chicago in ruins. Do you know what happened?
(answer: The Great Chicago Fire, which people said was started when Mrs. O'Leary's cow kicked over a lantern; Chicago)

Where? A gigantic rock formation towering 140' above the Illinois River stands in the middle of Starved Rock State Park. An Indian tribe was surrounded by enemies here. They climbed the rock, but were soon forced down because they had no food. Where is this historic park?
(answer: on the Illinois River near Ottawa)

Why? Abraham Lincoln and Stephen A. Douglas were both running for the senate. They campaigned in seven different Illinois towns by having debates (discussions). Why were these debates important to Lincoln even though he lost the election?
(answer: The nation's attention was focused on him, and he told people that he was against slavery; Springfield)

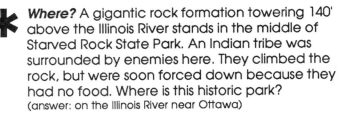

Make a movie in your mind. There are hundreds of coiled *springs* bouncing around in a large *field*. The springs are squeaking so much that they're making you *ill* with the *noise*. The springs in the field = Springfield, the capital of Illinois. Remember that you feel ill with the squeaky noise. Ill + noise = Illinois (pronounced without the "s," of course). It would be hard to forget that Springfield is the capital of Illinois, wouldn't it?

Ⓒ Ⓐ Ⓣ Ⓒ Ⓗ Ⓐ Ⓒ Ⓛ Ⓤ Ⓔ
Chicago's O'Hare Field is not the home for fast flying rabbits, but it is the busiest place in the U.S. for
(a) playing soccer
(b) playing football
(c) landing aircraft.
(answer: (c); clue: flying = aircraft)

ILLINOIS

HIP, HIP, HOORAY!

Little did Jean Pointe du Sable know when he built his small log cabin on the banks of the Chicago River what his property would be worth today. He set up a successful trading business, and 300 years later, the site of his modest cabin is in downtown Chicago. Historians believe that de Sable was originally from the island of Haiti. A midwest-sized cheer for the man who built the first permanent house in what is now Chicago. He founded one of America's great cities.

Did you know that only 10 percent of the energy used by a light bulb turns into light? Ouch! That's why it's hot. Start a light patrol in your house and see that every light is turned off when it's not needed. What should be done to the guilty party who leaves on lights? Perhaps you could make him or her put 5 or 10 cents into a family treat jar.

DID YOU KNOW ?

PUBLISHING GIANT

Chicagoan John Johnson has brought acclaim to Illinois as the leading publisher of America's best-selling magazines focused for a black audience. *Ebony* is an award-winning publication, and Johnson Publishing Company's other publications of *Jet, Ebony Jr.,* and *EM* are all magazine top sellers.

Ⓒ Ⓐ Ⓣ Ⓒ Ⓗ Ⓐ Ⓒ Ⓛ Ⓤ Ⓔ

Stick a feather in the cap of Joseph F. Glidden of DeKalb, Illinois, for he solved a prickly farm problem in 1873 by inventing
(a) automatic milking machines
(b) barbed wire
(c) egg candlers.
(answer (b); clue: prickly = barbed)

HOME SWEET HOME LINCOLN–STYLE

The log cabin where Lincoln grew up and the New Salem cabin where he studied law are all reminders that Lincoln and log cabins go together! How about building your own log cabin? *Here's what you need:* brown paper grocery bag, white glue, scissors, a full-length pencil, dark brown and black construction paper.

Here's what you do:

1. Cut 8 strips, 4" wide x 5" long, of the brown paper bag.

2. Roll the strips lengthwise around the pencil, forming logs. Glue the side down that is open.

3. Cut 8 more strips, 4" wide x 4" long, and repeat the process of rolling and gluing.

4. Arrange the logs with the longest ones as the sides of the cabin and the shorter ones as the front and back.

5. Glue them together by alternating the logs where they meet at the corners, starting with the first long, side logs.

6. Cut 4 or 5 more strips 4" wide for the front of the cabin, gradually getting smaller and smaller. These logs will be the part that tapers up to the top of the roof. Cut the exact same length logs for the back, using the same rolling, gluing process.

7. Starting with the longest logs, glue in place at the front and back of the cabin, making each log in front and back get shorter and shorter toward the top.

8. Fold the brown construction paper in half and "roof" your cabin. Cut to fit, and glue in place.

9. Cut a door and windows out of the black construction paper and glue in place.

We know what's on top of the ground in Illinois, but what's underneath? Are you surprised to know that there's coal under two-thirds of the state, and that it has the largest coal reserves in the U.S.? The coal is a soft coal called *bituminous*, and when it burns it causes a great deal of pollution. For this reason, not as much is mined now. Scientists are trying to figure out ways to keep it from harming our environment. Any ideas?

INDIANA

COLOR AMERICA!

With Larry Bird from French Lick, Indiana wearing the green of the NBA's Boston Celtics, and with the "Fighting Irish" of Notre Dame counting on a little shamrock good fortune once fall football comes around, what color comes to mind? Wouldn't a shamrock-colored green look great on your America! map?

What's a Hoosier? No one knows for sure how the name got started. The people of Indiana, the *Hoosier State*, can tell you that they're farmers, steel mill workers, oil drillers, and manufacturers. They're also fervent basketball players and fans, college football enthusiasts, and speed racing buffs. Movie and recording stars and T.V. personalities have called Indiana their home, and composers, poets, and authors have made Indiana proud. "The Crossroads of America" is the state's motto, and many people just passing through liked what they saw and stayed.

PICTURE THIS

Indiana looks like a top hat with ruffles on the bottom edge. Which President of the U.S. do you picture wearing a tall, black top hat? Of course, it's Abraham Lincoln. When Lincoln lived right next door in Illinois, do you think he bought his top hat in Indiana?

PACK YOUR BAGS

What do you do in a state that has lots of lakes and streams? For one thing, you could go to Crawfordsville and paddle a canoe with a friend in the annual Sugar Creek Canoe Race, or take in Washington Park in Michigan City. Its sandy beaches, picnicking areas, and zoo would feel like a day's vacation for anyone. The Indiana Sand Dunes are great fun in the summertime, and when covered with winter snows, it's a great place for cross-country skiing. Hoosiers know how to have fun!

THE CURIOUS W's

Who? My name goes with Notre Dame football, and I coached the "Fighting Irish" for 13 years. I also played football at Notre Dame, and I was especially known for my forward passes. I used clever football strategies to win 105 games, tie 5, and lose 12, while I was coach, but good sportsmanship was always more important to me than winning. Who am I?
(answer: Knute Rockne, born in Norway but lived in South Bend)

What? The premier auto race in the nation is held here every Memorial Day weekend. Hundreds of thousands of people are on hand to watch the

500- mile race that features 200 laps around the paved 2¹/₂ mile oval track. What is this famous track?
(answer: Indianapolis Motor Speedway; Indianapolis)

Where? You can see families here riding in horse-drawn carriages, because their religion forbids them to drive cars. They also cannot use electricity or go to war. Their heritage began in Switzerland, and today these Mennonite and Amish people carry on the farming traditions of their forefathers. Where do many Mennonite and Amish people live?
(answer: northeastern Indiana near Berne)

Why? It all started with John Studebaker making wheelbarrows for the gold miners in California. When he returned to South Bend, he and his brother made horse-drawn wagons. They eventually manufactured automobiles. Why was the Studebaker Company so important during World War II?
(answer: They made many of the amphibious vehicles and trucks for the U.S. military; South Bend)

How's your Latitude Attitude?

Are Indianapolis, Indiana and Valencia, Spain on the same approximate latitude (39°N) as Philadelphia, Pennsylvania or Cleveland, Ohio?

Make a movie in your mind. Imagine a large group of *Indians* dressed in colorful native costumes. Look more closely and you'll see the *Indian* chief juggling 100 *apples* at one time. Have you ever tried to juggle 3 apples? Tough, isn't it? Indians = Indiana, and the Indian chief juggling apples = Indianapolis, the capital. Indianapolis, Indiana.

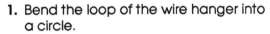
▪ ▪ ▪ ▪ ▪ ▪ ▪ BASKET BALL-OONS! ▪ ▪ ▪ ▪ ▪ ▪ ▪

For an indoor game that will always remind you of how much the Hoosiers love to play and watch basketball, give this a shot. *Here's what you need:* one wire coat hanger and several balloons.

Here's what you do:

1. Bend the loop of the wire hanger into a circle.

2. Hang it on a doorknob, bending the circle straight out from the door.

3. Blow up several balloons to a size that will fit through your wire basket.

4. Stand about 4' away and go for those free throws. This is even fun to play alone. Keep score, and when your field goal percentage gets too high, back up and try some 3-pointers!

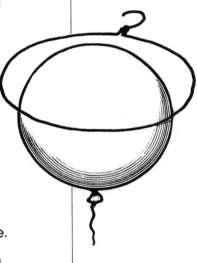

Ⓒ Ⓐ Ⓣ Ⓒ Ⓗ Ⓐ Ⓒ Ⓛ Ⓤ Ⓔ

William Henry Harrison led the battle against Tecumseh, the great Indian leader and defeated him in 1811, at
(a) the Skirmish of Gary
(b) the Battle of Tippecanoe
(c) the Siege of Fort Wayne.
(answer: (b); clue: battle = Battle)

C O L O R   A M E R I C A !

What does Iowa produce more of than any other place in the world? Hogs! And, it's from hogs that we get pork chops, bacon, sausage, and ham. To help remember Iowa's number one agriculture crop, hogs, a ham-colored light pink would most certainly get a squeal of delight on your America! map.

Flat farm lands with layers and layers of rich soil from ancient glaciers have made Iowa one of America's great agricultural states. It stands in a class by itself world-wide with its hog and corn production. Located between the mighty Mississippi and Missouri rivers, farming has been the prize winner of the state. Throughout lean years and bumper years, Iowa is tied to agriculture. The major industries — such giants as the largest tractor factory in the world, corn seed, animal feed, popcorn, breakfast cereal, and meat-packing plants — are clearly farm related. The *Hawkeye State* holds a place of distinction in America.

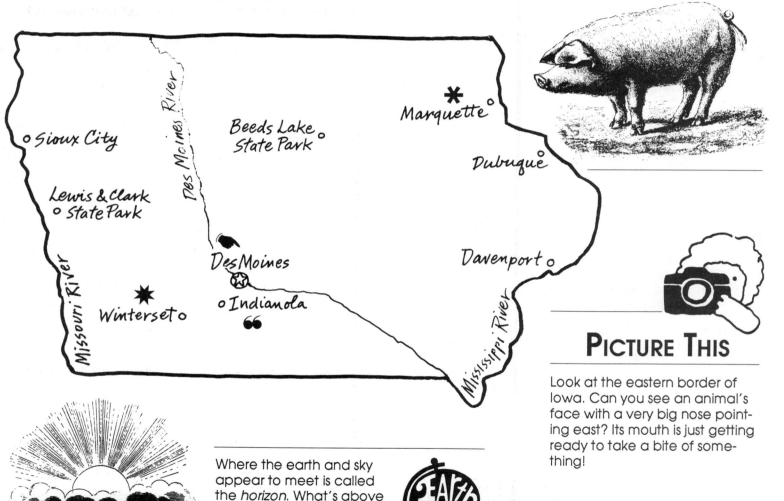

Sioux City

Beeds Lake State Park

Marquette

Dubuque

Des Moines River

Lewis & Clark State Park

Missouri River

Des Moines

Davenport

Winterset

Indianola

Mississippi River

PICTURE THIS

Look at the eastern border of Iowa. Can you see an animal's face with a very big nose pointing east? Its mouth is just getting ready to take a bite of something!

Where the earth and sky appear to meet is called the *horizon*. What's above the horizon in the daytime and below the horizon at night? It must be the sun.

EARTH TALK

Make a movie in your mind. Picture a man with three *coins* in one *eye*. The coins are arranged in the shape of a *"D."* The capital of Iowa is yours. Eye = Iowa, and "D" + coins sounds like Des Moines. Des Moines, Iowa.

THE CURIOUS W's

 Who? I was an Iowa farm boy long before I rode the range in cowboy movies on the motion picture screen. Two of my most popular movies were *She Wore a Yellow Ribbon*, and *True Grit*. In fact, I won the Academy Award for best actor for my role in *True Grit*. Who am I?
(answer: John Wayne; Winterset)

 What? For a glimpse of what farming was like in the 1800s, you can see it all here. The guides, dressed in historical clothing, take you through Iowa's farming history. This 600-acre attraction also has a farm of the future. What is this museum and exhibition site called?
(answer: Living History Farms; near Des Moines)

 Where? Many of the prehistoric Indian mounds are shaped like wolves, snakes, bears, and birds. Some of them are up to 300' long, and one is shaped like a giant woman. The Mound Builders built these earthen mounds at a site which is now known as Effigy Mounds National Monument near Marquette. Where is Marquette?

 Why? Indianola is not a large city, but thousands of people flock here each year for a special event. There's also a museum with exhibits that would be hard to match. Why is Indianola such an attraction?
(answer: The National Hot Air Balloon Championship is held here, at the National Balloon Museum. Did you know we had such a thing in the U.S.?)

 WHO SAID THAT?

What U.S. President said, "A chicken in every pot"? It was Herbert Hoover.

IOWA

One unusual group of Iowa soldiers who fought in the Civil War for the Union were nicknamed the "Greybeards." Rightly so, because not one man in the group was under 45 years old, and some of the soldiers were in their seventies. Isn't it interesting that some of the men had their own grandchildren serving in the army with them? These "Greybeards" did not fight on the battlefronts, but they served their country well by acting as guards for the Confederate prisoners. A 21-gun salute to the "Greybeards"!

PACK YOUR BAGS

One of the major highlights of the year in the *Hawkeye State* is the Iowa State Fair held during the month of August in Des Moines. There's stiff competition for the blue ribbons in every possible category of agriculture. Young people from all over the state exhibit their prized farm animals. There are games, sports competitions, heaps and barrels of farm-fresh produce, fresh baked-goods, and lots of mouth-watering food for those hearty midwest appetites. There are rides galore and entertainment, too. No wonder Iowans plan their vacations around the month of August.

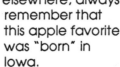

DID YOU KNOW?

When you eat a red, juicy Delicious apple, you're enjoying it because of a shocking event that happened in the community of Peru, Iowa one night. During a lightning storm, Jesse Hiatt's apple tree was struck by a bolt of lightning, and the tree was destroyed. When new trees began to grow from the shoots of that tree, something was different about the apples. They had little nubs at the bottom and were not like any apple ever seen before. One of Jesse Hiatt's friends tried one and said it was "delicious." The name stuck and even though most Delicious Apples are grown elsewhere, always remember that this apple favorite was "born" in Iowa.

ⒸⒶⓉⒸⒽ Ⓐ ⒸⓁⓊⒺ

The 31st President, Herbert Hoover, was born in West Branch, Iowa. He was the first president to
(a) be born west of the Mississippi
(b) have an honorary doctorate from a major college
(c) have three vice presidents.
(answer: (a); clue: West = west)

An Iowa Treat: Easy Baked Caramel Corn

Iowa takes undisputed first place in the nation for pork production, but it also leads the states in the production of corn. Whether you roast it, pop it, steam it, or bake it, corn has been an American favorite since the Indians introduced it to the early colonists. It just so happens that this Easy Baked Caramel Corn will turn just about anyone into a corn lover. Ask an adult for help around the stove.

Here's what you need:

2	**sticks margarine**
2	**cups firmly packed light brown sugar**
1/2	**cup light corn syrup**
1	**teaspoon salt**
1/2	**teaspoon baking soda**
1	**teaspoon vanilla**
6	**quarts popped popcorn**

Here's what you do:

1. Melt margarine over low heat in a sauce pan. Stir in brown sugar, corn syrup, and salt.

2. Bring to a boil, stirring constantly. Boil without stirring for 5 minutes.

3. Remove from heat and stir in baking soda and vanilla.

4. Gradually pour over popped popcorn, mixing well.

5. Turn into two large shallow baking or roasting pans, spreading out evenly.

6. Bake in 225° oven for 30 minutes, being careful to stir it and turn it over every 10 minutes with a metal spatula.

7. Remove from oven and immediately dump onto waxed paper. Cool and break into chunks. Store in tightly covered container....that is, if there is any left to store.

DID YOU KNoW?

Farm animals don't eat the same kind of corn that we slather with butter and call corn-on-the-cob. Instead, farm animals, who do eat lots of corn (off the cob, of course), eat a completely different variety of corn that is grown for feed. People eat sweet corn. Popcorn is another variety of corn that is grown specifically to be popped. Would you be surprised to know that Iowa is our leading corn producer?

"Oh, give me a home, where the buffalo roam" . . . was once a perfect description of Kansas when herds of bison thundered across the plains. "Home on the Range" is the state song, but the buffalo are gone and the range is where the people used to live. Located midway between the Atlantic and Pacific oceans, Kansas has been called the "Bread basket of America" because of its premier grain production of corn in the east, wheat in the west, and its many flour mills. With its grassy plains, rolling farms, grain elevators, oil derricks, and tall buildings, the landscape of Kansas is changing.

Sunflowers are the tall, yellow wildflowers that grow on the plains of Kansas. Have you ever eaten sunflower seeds? The center of the sunflower has hundreds of little seeds, and when they're dried, baked, and salted, they make a wonderful treat. Kansas is called the *Sunflower State*, because of its yellow prairie flowers. How do you think Kansas would look a bright, sunny yellow on your America! map?

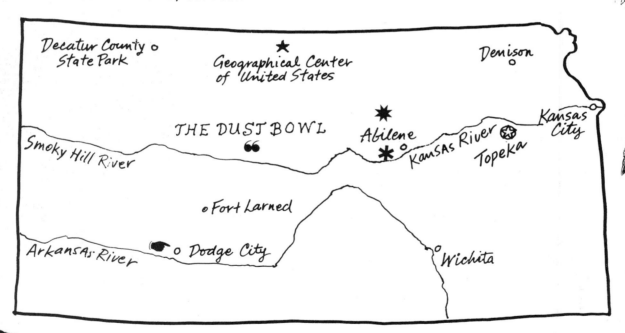

Decatur County State Park

Geographical Center of United States

Denison

THE DUST BOWL

Smoky Hill River

Abilene

Kansas River

Topeka

Kansas City

Fort Larned

Arkansas River

Dodge City

Wichita

PICTURE THIS

Kansas looks like a rectangle with a little piece of the rectangle torn on the northeast corner. Can you see it?

THE CURIOUS W's

Who? I was one of seven boys in my family. We were poor, and I worked from the time I was very young, mostly at a creamery. I didn't know when I graduated from West Point that I would someday become a five-star general. I also had no idea that I would ever become president of the United States. In grade school I was nicknamed "Little Ike." Do you know my real name?
(answer: Dwight David Eisenhower, 34th President of the United States, born in Denison, Texas, raised in Abilene)

 What? "The Cowboy Capital of the World" is how this wild western cattle town was known. With famous lawmen such as Wyatt Earp, Wild Bill Hickok, and Bat Masterson trying to keep the peace, stories and legends about outlaws, shootouts, cattle drives, and Miss Kitty and the Long Branch Saloon make it one of America's favorite western landmarks. What is the name of the town where you can still see where the action took place?
(answer: Dodge City)

 Where? It's only a replica of what it once was during the frontier days when great herds of longhorn cattle were driven across the old Chisholm Trail, across Texas to the rails of Kansas. A boulder on the lawn in front of the post office marks the spot where this famous trail ended. Abilene was the first of the Kansas cow towns. Can you find it on the map?

 Why? No rain, and powdery, dry topsoil were all that was needed when strong winds whipped across part of the Great Plains into Kansas during the 1930s. Crops were actually blown away and the great clouds of dust forced farmers to leave their homes and land. This region was known as the Dust Bowl. Why is it important?
(answer: New methods of planting and farming were developed and trees were planted as wind breaks.)

 Make a movie in your mind. Picture a large *can* in the middle of the street. You are ready to play the game kick-the-can, but oh, dear, there's a hole in your shoe, and your *toe's* peeking out to see what it's going to kick. Wham! Too late. Can = Kansas, and toe + peek = Topeka, the capital of Kansas. Topeka, Kansas.

 Colorful rodeos, fairs, and festivals are reminders of Kansas' early frontier days, and they can be found nearly everywhere in the state at any season. Turtle races, river festivals, a Mexican fiesta, and Indian powwows highlight the summer months, and if you want to visit a real fort to have a glimpse of old U.S. cavalry bases, there's plenty to see.

■ LOWLANDS, PRAIRIES, AND PLAINS ■

There's a stretch of land 1,500 miles across, between the Appalachian and the Rocky Mountains, that is called the central low lands. Prairies and plains, as you know, are other names given to these lowlands. Look at a map of the United States and locate The Great Plain. Here's a hint: it's west of the Mississippi River.

 Kansans know when to head for their cellars, thanks to the National Weather Service. Kansas records more tornadoes than any other state.
A tornado watch: cautions people that a current storm could possibly contain tornadoes and to be on the lookout.
A tornado warning: alerts people that a tornado has been sighted or detected by radar, so be prepared.
A tornado: the destructive funnel-shaped whirlwind, about 300 yards across that twists and skips across the land. It can dart back up into the black cloud above, and then suddenly dip down and touch the earth. Only when it touches the earth is it destructive.

KANSAS

"Toto, I've a feeling we're not in Kansas anymore . . ." were Dorothy's first words when she opened the door of her Kansas farm house in *The Wizard of Oz*. Children all over the world know the name of Kansas without having any idea where it is. You know, don't you?

HIP, HIP, HOORAY!

Howland Island in the Pacific Ocean was her refueling destination, but she never made it, and her disappearance has been a mystery since it happened in 1937. The first woman to fly across the Atlantic Ocean alone, Amelia Earhart of Atchison, is recognized as the best-known woman aviator in the world. She was the first woman to fly from Honolulu to the mainland, and the first woman to fly across the United States in both directions. A salute and dip of the wing to Amelia Earhart, an American aviation pioneer.

Dorothy's Kansas

The Gale farm in Kansas is no doubt, the most famous farm in the world even though it's only make-believe. Uncle Henry, Aunt Em, their niece, Dorothy, and farm hands, Zeke, Hunk, and Hickory come to life in L. Frank Baum's story, *The Wizard of Oz*. Sharpen up your pencil, map skills, and imagination and see if you can do this: Using a large sheet of butcher paper, poster board, or just plain white typing paper which you can tape together on the back as you go, create your own Gale farm in Kansas. Don't forget the pig sty and the water pump, the chickens, and Toto, too. Are you going to show the cyclone, off in the distance? What about old Miss Almira Gulch riding on her bicycle with the basket on the back?

For a real movie-like set design, you can take this a step further. Remember in the movie how the farm scene is only in black and white? Why not do your map the same way, and then make an entire layout of the Land of Oz, all in color? You can decide where to put such landmarks as Munchkinland, the Witch's Castle, and the Emerald City, itself. Don't forget the Yellow Brick Road, or the bright orange poppies, the dark forest, and the locations where Dorothy and Toto meet the Scarecrow, Tin Man, and the Cowardly Lion. This could turn into quite a mural. Little extras like glitter, foil for water, cut paper, real straw, and anything else imaginable will make your map seem as real as the movie . . . "Just follow the Yellow Brick Road."

KENTUCKY

Legends of Daniel Boone, the pathfinder, alerted everyone to the natural beauty of Kentucky. Steven Foster's "My Old Kentucky Home," the state song, also tells us of the genteel country life of yesteryear. Kentucky's many rivers, temperate climate, and abundant rainfall give nature the moisture it needs to produce brilliant flowering plants growing wild through-out the state. From the eastern and western coal field regions to the miles of\rolling horse farms of the Blue-grass, Kentucky has a personality and charm unlike any of our other states.

Kentucky is the *Bluegrass State*, and you may wonder if Kentucky's grass is really blue. The grass is thick and lush, but it's a deep, velvety green and not blue. In the early springtime these native grasses produce tiny little blue flowers so that from a distance the grass does indeed, look blue. Green for the lush wild grasses, or blue for the delicate little flowers? You decide which color would look best on your America! map.

Louisville

Fort Knox

Frankfort

Lexington

Boonesborough

Ohio River

Mammoth Cave National Park

Cumberland Gap

Paducah

PICTURE THIS

Can you see that Kentucky looks like a little fish swimming toward the east? That little fish has lots and lots of fins across the top of its back, doesn't it? And it's swimming right between West Virginia and Virginia, heading for the Atlantic Ocean.

Kentucky says, "Happy Birthday" to two of its most distinguished and popular birth-staters. Abraham Lincoln was born in Hodgenville, and his wife, Mary Todd Lincoln, was born in Lexington. Did you know that both Lincolns were Kentuckians?

When the Civil War ended in 1865, many people were still in a fighting mood. The Hatfield family of West Virginia and their neighbors, the McCoy family from Kentucky, started a feud that lasted for over thirty years! Can you imagine being that angry with anyone for all that time? The Hatfields were loyal to the South, and the McCoys supported Lincoln and the Union. Many of their family members were killed in the quarreling before later generations of the families called a truce. The Hatfields and the McCoys were probably America's most famous feuding families.

GROW YOUR OWN STALAGMITES

With Kentucky's vast mineral wealth in coal and limestone caves, here's an unusual project you'll enjoy watching grow.

Here's what you need:

Glass bowl
Food coloring
Pieces of charcoal (not the kind pre-soaked with lighter fluid), porous brick, cement, or an old sponge
Regular table salt
Small amount of laundry bluing*

Here's what you do:

1. Put the charcoal (or whatever you are using to grow the crystals on) in a shallow, glass bowl.

2. Sprinkle two tablespoons each of water, salt, and laundry bluing over the base material.

3. The next day, add two more tablespoons of salt.

4. On the third day, pour two tablespoons each of salt, water, and bluing into the bottom of the bowl (not over the charcoal).

5. Now add a few drops of food coloring to each piece of charcoal or brick. Keep in a dry, airy place.

* Most supermarkets carry laundry bluing, or write to Mrs. Stewart's Bluing, P.O. Box 201405, Bloomington, MN 55420.

THE CURIOUS W's

 Who? I'm easily recognizable by the coonskin cap I wear, but many other frontiersmen of my time wore them, too. I explored much of Kentucky, and I started a settlement at Boonesborough. The trail I blazed is called the Wilderness Road. Coonskin cap? Boonesborough? Wilderness Road? I think you know who I am.
(answer: Daniel Boone; founder of Boonesborough)

 What? America's premier and world renown horse racing event of the year is held at Churchill Downs on the first Saturday of May. The first race was held in 1875 and the 1¼ mile track is now one of the fastest in the world. What is the name of this famous "Run for the Roses" event?

(answer: the Kentucky Derby, Churchill Downs; Louisville)

 Where? An underground sea? Underground lakes and rivers that you can navigate? Is this possible? It is when you're in this world famous national park. Mammoth Cave National Park with over 150 miles of winding passageways is the largest cave system in the world. Do you know where this magnificent natural wonder is located?
(answer: northeast of Bowling Green)

 Why? This granite, steel, and concrete building has one of the tightest security systems in the nation. It's located on an army post outside of Louisville, and in 1936, the U.S. Treasury Department made it the richest building in America. Why is Fort Knox important?
(answer: It's where the United States' gold reserves are kept. . .no visitors!)

 Make a movie in your mind. Imagine your *kin* (relatives) *tucking* you in bed, and where is this bed? It's right in the middle of a *fort*. What are the walls of the fort made of? *Franks* (hot dogs)! Now you know the capital of Kentucky. Kin + tucking = Kentucky, and franks + fort = Frankfort. Frankfort, Kentucky. (What if the fort caught on fire? It sure would taste good! Pass the mustard.)

 Of course, Kentucky has its wonderful variety of fairs and sports, but a most interesting visit is going to see one of Kentucky's coal mines. We've used coal for fuel for hundreds of years. The United States is the second largest producer of coal in the world, next to China, and Kentucky has supplied much of that resource. But what has coal mining done to Kentucky? Deep mines were built into the Kentucky mountains and miners have risked their lives for years going underground, working in dangerous situations. Mines are safer today, but the work is still hard and dangerous.

Two other mining methods are being used: *Strip mining* — whole tops of mountains and hills are removed or "stripped" to get to the coal. By law, mine owners who use this method are required to replace and restore what has been damaged. *Auger mining* — huge drills bore into the underground coal, and then the coal comes out on a rotating conveyor belt. To get to the coal seams, heavy road grading equipment clears off entire mountains.

There are hundreds of years of coal left to mine in Kentucky. What about the land? After years of neglect, conservationists are now working hard to help restore the coal-mining regions of Kentucky to the beautiful, mountainous, wildlife region that it once was.

 **CATCH A CLUE**
The city of Louisville can be very proud of one of its claims to fame which is
(a) oldest city university in the U.S.
(b) home of the first horse race in the U.S.
(c) the first concrete road in U.S.A.
(answer: (a); clue: city = city)

 WHO SAID THAT? How would you feel if you ran for president and lost three times? Henry Clay from Kentucky did just that, but he went on to become one of America's great statesmen. When someone once asked him how he felt about his many losses, he replied, "I had rather be right than be president."

This may be a tough decision, but if you could pick just one color for a brand new car, what color would you choose? If you color Michigan your favorite car color, it will help to remind you that more cars are made in Michigan than in any other U.S. state. Have you decided?

Isle Royale National Park

Porcupine Mts. State Park

LAKE SUPERIOR

Sault Ste Marie

Straits of Mackinac

LAKE HURON

LAKE MICHIGAN

The Great Lakes, extensive river waterways, and rich natural resources of iron ore and lumber determined the future of Michigan. Factories lured people away from their farms, and soon, the *Wolverine State* became a giant of industry. Beautiful forests cover over half of the state and four of the five Great Lakes touch its borders. There are thousands of islands, numerous cascading waterfalls, and some of the country's largest herds of deer, elk, and moose. Michigan has the best of two worlds — the great pillars of American industry and some of the most scenic natural landscapes in our nation.

Ludington State Park

Flint

Pontiac

Lansing

Holland

Detroit

Battle Creek

Dearborn

LAKE ERIE

PICTURE THIS

Michigan is divided into two separate parts. The largest part of the state could be a mitten with the thumb on the east. The part of the state that is smaller looks like a shark swimming away from the hand with the mitten, going west. Isn't it fun what you can see when you use your imagination to picture things?

THE CURIOUS W's

✴ **Who?** I changed the course of transportation in America when I began putting cars together on moving assembly lines. We could complete a new car in less than a minute with this new method of mass production, and because of it, I could sell my new Model T cars for under $300! Who am I?
(answer: Henry Ford; Dearborn)

✳ **Where?** There are no cars allowed, but you can walk, hike, bicycle, ride a horse, or ride in a horse-drawn carriage around this scenic resort island. Old Fort Mackinac is the largest summer hotel in the world, and it really was once a fort. Can you find Mackinac Island?
(answer: Find the Straits of Mackinac)

❝ **Why?** Lake Huron is 26 feet lower than its neighbor, Lake Superior, so a canal called the Soo Locks was built at Sault Sainte Marie. Do you know why this canal is so vital to America's shipping?
(answer: The Soo Locks connect the two lakes by raising or lowering the water level so that barges and ships can go from one lake to another; Sault Sainte Marie)

DESIGN • A • CAR

Who said that only boys can design and draw cars? Surprise! Some of Detroit's best car designers are women, so here's a project that everybody will enjoy. Think futuristic. Think sleek and fast. Think of a new car design that will use a new kind of fuel and get great mileage. Who knows. . .someday you may end up at a drawing board in Detroit, Flint, Pontiac, or Lansing. For your papier-mache car of the future, *here's what you need:* newspapers torn into 1" x 4" strips; containers for mixing; glue mixture of 1 cup water to 1 cup flour mixed well until it's creamy and thick (or liquid wallpaper paste or prepared papier-mache glue); aluminum foil; paint brushes; tape; tempera or acrylic paints; acrylic clear spray; small cardboard boxes (jewelry-sized for the body of the car base).
Here's what you do:

1. Use the little cardboard boxes, or tape pieces of cardboard together, to get the basic car body.

2. Loosely start crushing the foil over and around the cardboard, until your car starts taking the shape you want. By pushing and pressing the foil, it will shape quite nicely.

3. Dip paper strips into the glue and start covering your car form. Let dry thoroughly between layers.

4. When the glue is dry, add details of glued-on cardboard shapes or any other materials. Consider little mirror pieces or foil for headlights and windows.

5. Paint your car.

6. Spray with clear acrylic when paint is dry for that Detroit-new car finish.

MICHIGAN

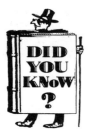

It's easy to remember the five Great Lakes. Picture many homes along the lake shores and think of the word HOMES: H = Huron, O = Ontario, M = Michigan, E = Erie, and S = Superior. Easy, right?

PACK YOUR BAGS

If you were blindfolded and then stood in front of Sleeping Bear and had the blindfold removed, what would you expect to see? An Indian chief? Maybe a real bear at a zoo? It's for sure you'd be surprised to be staring at a massive, towering sand dune. Where are the camels? You might think you're in the Sahara Desert, but Sleeping Bear is located on the shoreline of Lake Michigan. Would you be adventurous enough to climb to the top? If you climbed to the top, how would you get down? Walk, slide, roll? Can you believe that some people have actually skied down from the top!

LIGHTS, CAMERA, ACTION!

Make a movie in your mind. A *lance* (spear) is *zing*ing through the air. Where's it going? It's headed straight for the opening of a giant squirt *gun*. Remember Michigan when you picture the squirt gun. Gun = Michigan. And how have you pictured Lansing, the state capital? It's a lance that is zinging though the air! Lance + zing = Lansing. Lansing, Michigan.

HIP, HIP, HOORAY!

What would breakfast be like without the munchies and crunchies? Before the early 1900s, you might have eaten hot oatmeal for your breakfast cereal, but thanks to Dr. John Harvey Kellogg, inventor of corn and wheat flakes, you now have an overwhelming choice of cereals. Grocery shelves are stacked with boxes of cold cereals with mind-boggling names. The doctor's younger brother, Will, started the company that is now the Kellogg Company. At about the same time, Charles Post invented Grape Nuts. Today, Kellogg's, Post, and other Battle Creek cereal makers keep kids smiling before they grab their book bags and head for school. What's your favorite cereal? Is it made in Battle Creek?

Lake Superior is the world's biggest lake - a little larger than South Carolina. Since the U.S. and Canada use Lake Superior for all kinds of shipping and industry, both countries are working very hard to clean up the lake's water.

JUST IMAGINE

A $25,000 prize was just too much for the young aviator who was a U.S. Air Mail Service pilot to pass up. To win the money, you had to be the first person to fly non-stop from New York to Paris. Charles Lindberg, who was born in Detroit, was determined to win the prize. In the single-engine Spirit of St. Louis, he took off from Roosevelt Field in Garden City, New York, and 33½ hours later, he landed at Le Bourget Field outside Paris. Can you imagine what it was like to fly a small, single-wing, single-engine plane that distance without today's sophisticated instruments or even a radio? When he stepped from his plane, he was stunned to see over 100,000 people screaming and shouting their congratulations. The "Lone Eagle" had landed and made aviation history. The date was May 21, 1927. Just imagine.

We all know that Canada is our friendly neighbor to the north. Curious, isn't it that part of Canada is SOUTH of Michigan. Check it out. It's true. Another interesting geo fact is that Michigan is our only state that is separated into two parts.

HIP, HIP, HOORAY!

★ ★ ★ ★ ★ ★

Have you ever sold newspapers or had a paper route? One of our great Americans, born in Detroit, started earning a living as a paper boy. He eventually became a member of the United Nations, and he played a major part in bringing peace to Palestine. For his hard work, in 1950, he became the very first black person to receive the Nobel peace prize. His name is Ralph Johnson Bunche. Three cheers for Mr. Bunche, a fine person, indeed!

★ ★

CATCH A CLUE

Henry Ford and Ransom E. Olds produced a gasoline-powered car in the year 1896. Two great car companies developed from these two pioneers.

(a) Oldsmobile and Ford
(b) Pontiac and Plymouth
(c) Cadillac and Buick

(answer: (a); clue: Ford and Olds = Oldsmobile and Ford)

MINNESOTA

Cinderella's slipper was glass, but have you heard of a lady's slipper that is pink and white and not really a slipper at all? Minnesota's state flower is the rare, pink and white orchid called a lady's slipper. It will be a challenge to decide how to color Minnesota on your America! map. All pink? White? Maybe a combination of both would remind you of this delicate wildflower.

Minnesota may have more lakes than it has gophers, and more lakes and gophers than one can count, because it is known as the *Land of 10,000 Lakes* and the *Gopher State*. It is famous for its twins — the Twin Cities of Minneapolis and St. Paul, and for its American League baseball team, the Minnesota Twins. A state of vast natural resources, it's also an undisputed winner in some of the most magnificent wilderness areas of America.

PACK YOUR BAGS

Minnesota cares about keeping its wilderness as wilderness. Think about it. No bottles or cans, no motor boats, no campfires. When you paddle a canoe on one of the 1,200 miles of icy streams of the Boundary Waters Canoe Area, you could very well be an Indian or a fur trapper 300 years ago. You'll see much of the same scenery. What does BWCA stand for? Can you guess? Would you like to canoe in such a wilderness? What a great experience! Thank you, Minnesota.

PICTURE THIS

Picture a ski boot. The bottom of the boot is flat, the back of the boot is straight, and the toe is rounded, pointing east. You can even see the tongue of the boot which is sticking out towards the east. Picture your foot going into the boot from Canada. Now you know the shape of Minnesota.

THE CURIOUS W's

Who? I was a U.S. Senator, and vice-president of the United States. I ran for the office of president, but I lost by a very narrow margin to Richard Nixon in 1968. Do you know my name?
(answer: Hubert Humphrey; born in South Dakota but resided in Minneapolis)

 What? Indians carved peace pipes from the deep red stone. It is so rare that it's found only in quarries in one area of the state. What is its very appropriate name?
(answer: pipestone; near Pipestone)

Why? The water that flows out of Lake Itasca in northwest Minnesota is cold, clear, and less than two feet deep. It's about ten feet wide, and when it was located in 1832 by an American, why was it such a major discovery?
(answer: It's the source of the Mississippi River; northwestern part of the state.)

ONLY 10,000 LAKES?????????????

How many lakes are in Minnesota? A state nickname says that there are 10,000, but that's about 5,000 short of the real count. There are so many lakes in Minnesota that many of them have the exact same names. How many lakes would you guess are called Long Lake? Would you believe an astonishing 90, at least!

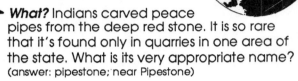

Make a movie in your mind. You're lost on a desert. Along comes a boy with a wheelbarrow filled with *mini* cans of *soda*. You are so thrilled to see him, that you tell him he must be a *saint*. He says that he is just a boy named *Paul*. My, what a good person he is! Saint + Paul = St. Paul, the capital, and mini + soda = Minnesota. St. Paul, Minnesota.

It builds bridges, buildings, battleships, cars, and even the pots and pans we use for cooking. It is steel, and to make steel there must be iron ore. Minnesota's iron ore from the Mesabi, Cuyuna, and Vermillion ranges produces over 60 percent of this valuable natural resource in the nation.

• EXPLORING YOUR ROOTS •

Do you know where your ancestors came from? Do you know what their traditions were? These are good things to discover. Make a chart of 4 generations. You are the first generation; your parents are the second generation. Your grandparents on both sides are the third, and, of course, your great grandparents are the fourth generation. If you can't find this information, your state has a *genealogical society* to help you, or you could contact the huge L.D.S. Genealogical Society in Utah that has branches in every state. You can learn about your roots, appreciate your heritage, and maybe learn something about other parts of your country and other countries, as well.

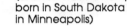 

CATCH A CLUE

In the year 1889, William and his two sons established this famous clinic in Rochester, Minnesota. The name of this clinic is
(a) The Salk Institute
(b) The Sabin Center
(c) The Mayo Clinic
(answer: (c); clue: clinic = Clinic)

MISSOURI

The *Show Me State* has given America great inventors, scientists, statesmen, a president, writers, poets, sports heroes, artists, manufacturers, and musicians. It's also given all of us a wealth of natural beauty. The wooded Ozark Highlands is the last, large forested area, before the plains and prairies heading West. Their beauty is still viewed by thousands of tourists each year just as it was in days of old. Home to the two greatest rivers of America — the Mississippi and the Missouri, Missourians continue to show America what they can do.

Bluebirds and bluejays love Missouri and so do Canada geese and bald eagles, who spend their winters in wildlife refuges. The official state bird is the bluebird, and all Missouri birds would donate a feather to your cap if you colored Missouri blue on your America! map.

St. Joseph

Hannibal

Kansas City

Missouri River

Independence

St. Louis

Jefferson City

Springfield

^ ^ ^ ^ ^
^ ^ ^ Mts ^
Ozark ^ ^ ^

Mark Twain
National Forest

Mississippi River

Land formed by the deposit of clay and silt at the mouth of a river is called a *delta*. Can you recall such a delta? Yes, the Mississippi.

PICTURE THIS

The southeast end of Missouri seems to have a funnel coming out and draining the rest of the state. It's probably water from the Missouri and Mississippi rivers.

DID YOU KNoW ?

Missouri has more known caves than any other state in the U.S. Over 45,000 caves have been identified and recorded, and each year more are added to the list. Does your state have any caves? Can you name them?

THE CURIOUS W's

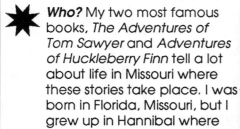

Who? My two most famous books, *The Adventures of Tom Sawyer* and *Adventures of Huckleberry Finn* tell a lot about life in Missouri where these stories take place. I was born in Florida, Missouri, but I grew up in Hannibal where my real name was Samuel Langhorne Clemens. I think you'll know me better by my pen name. Who am I?
(answer: Mark Twain; Hannibal)

What? It is located at what was once a stopping and starting place for early Indians and explorers, pioneers, trappers, and settlers. The site was used by thousands to cross the Mississippi River and head for trails leading West. What is the towering structure that marks this special location?
(answer: Gateway Arch; St. Louis)

Where? Relays of expert riders carried mail across the country by a system known as the Pony Express. It started in St. Joseph, Missouri; Sacramento, California was the end of the trail. Can you locate the home of the Pony Express?
(answer: St. Joseph)

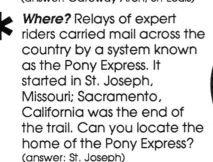

1860 1861
PONY EXPRESS

LIGHTS, CAMERA, ACTION!

Make a movie in your mind. Look up in the sky and what do you see? It's a *missile* soaring over your house. Why is the missile soaring over your house? Because Thomas *Jefferson's kitty* set it off. Imagine Thomas Jefferson telling his kitty not to set off any more soaring missiles. Missile + soaring = Missouri, and Jefferson + kitty = Jefferson City, its capital. Jefferson City, Missouri.

TOM SAWYER
BY
MARK TWAIN

WHO SAID THAT?

When a congressman from Missouri was getting tired of hearing his fellow congressmen always brag about their states, Willard Vandiver spoke up and said, "I come from a country that raises corn, cotton, cockleburs, and Democrats. I'm from Missouri and you have to show me!" Missourians liked what he said, and the state has been known as the *Show Me State* ever since.

SHOW ME

CATCH A CLUE

The Harry S. Truman Library in Independence, Missouri has the document of surrender that ended World War II. This document was signed on board the U.S.S.
(a) Arizona
(b) Utah
(c) Missouri.
(answer: (c); clue: Missouri = Missouri)

MISSOURI

★ ALL-AMERICAN DELIGHTS ★

Two of America's favorites, hot dogs and ice cream cones, made their very first appearance ever at the 1904 World's Fair in St. Louis. Little kids and big kids everywhere are very appreciative.

Want to explore a cave like Tom Sawyer and Huckleberry Finn did? You can do that. Want to drift down a river like Tom and Huck did in their stories? You can do that, too. You can also fish, hike, and swim. No wonder Tom and Huck had so much fun. Missouri is a great place for outdoor recreation with its many rivers, streams, and lakes. There's even a lake named Mark Twain!

PACK YOUR BAGS

HIP, HIP, HOORAY!

Mothers may cry when they read one on Mother's Day; Dad's chuckle on Father's Day, and kids can't wait to see who signed theirs on their birthdays. There's a grand selection for nearly every imaginable holiday and occasion of the year. Missourian Joyce Clyde Hall and his Hallmark greeting cards are a favorite American tradition and the largest greeting card manufacturer in the world.

CATCH A CLUE

The St. Louis World's Fair in 1904 was more than just fun and games. It commemorated the centennial of the Louisiana Purchase. Another important event took place at the Exposition, which was
(a) the Olympic Games
(b) the first Arabian horse show
(c) the U.S. Open Golf Tournament
(answer: (a); clue, games = Games)

WANTED DEAD OR ALIVE

Frontier towns attracted notorious outlaws because there weren't enough U.S. marshals to go around in the early days of westward expansion. Missouri bandits and gunslingers, like brothers Frank and Jesse James, were pictured on "wanted" posters throughout the country. Belle Starr, the Daltons, and the Younger Brothers also made Missouri their home until one by one, the outlaws either left the state, were jailed, or killed. Missouri did a good job of getting rid of its bad men and women.

WESTWARD HO!

Westward Ho! Be a pioneer for the day and make an authentic-looking covered wagon, since St. Louis was a starting point for many of the pioneers heading West. You might want to make some miniature "goods" for your trek. *Here's what you need:* a small rectangular box or a shoe box for a larger wagon; bendable wire or pipe cleaners; piece of cloth; heavy paper; cardboard for wheels; felt pens, crayons, paints.
Here's what you do:

1. Color, paint, or cover the outside of the box with construction paper.

2. Bend 5 pipe cleaners or wires from one side of the box to the other to make the bows. Tape in place inside the box.

3. Cover the bows with cloth and then cut to the shape, tucking extra material down inside the bed (box) of the wagon. Cut cardboard wheels and draw in spokes with pens or crayons. Glue two on each side of the wagon bed. If you want the wheels to turn, attach with a pin or piece of wire that you bend over inside the box. Now what will you decide to put inside the wagon?

With fields of golden kernels of corn, golden ripe wheat, and wild goldenrod, Nebraska's state flower, what would be more fitting than a rich golden color for Nebraska on your America! map?

The Great Plains means farming and grasses, and Nebraska has more varieties of grass than any other state in the nation. Where there's grass there are bound to be animals grazing, and the *Cornhusker State* is a leading cattle and hog producer. It's home to the largest cattle market and meat-packing center in the entire world. And don't forget the grain. Corn, wheat, and rye crops from Nebraska help feed the nation and other countries of the world. Check your cereal boxes for names of grains, and chances are, you're eating something grown in Nebraska. The state song says that Nebras-kans are proud of their beautiful "peaceful prairieland. Laced with many rivers and the hills of sand; dark green valleys cradled in the earth . . ."

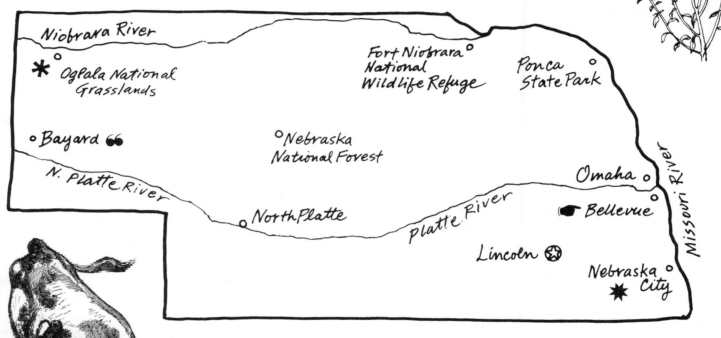

PICTURE THIS

Have you ever seen a picture of an old pirate ship with the cannon mounted on the deck? Nebraska looks like one of those old, big barreled cannons, ready to fire west. What a big shot!

THE CURIOUS W's

Who? I lost the election for first governor of the state of Nebraska, but I helped the state in another way. I began planting trees on some property I owned along the Missouri River, and I campaigned vigorously to convince others to plant trees in our state. Arbor Day was started in my honor, and today it is celebrated in many states across the nation. Who am I?
(answer: Julius Morton; born in New York, but lived most of his life in Nebraska City)

What? Offutt Air Force Base is home to one of America's most important defense systems. At a nearby museum there are aircraft, missiles, shows, and displays, and a "red alert" reenactment is staged to show visitors what it would be like if our country were under attack. What is this military defense system?

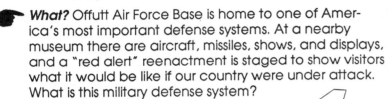

(answer: Strategic Air Command (SAC); Bellevue)

Where? Curious isn't it that the peculiar rock formations look like bodies of prehistoric monsters and dinosaurs if you use your imagination. Toadstool Park actually is a site where many prehistoric animal fossils have been found. Can you find this bizarre-looking area?
(answer: Oglala National Grasslands, north of Crawford)

Why? Pointing skyward like a giant stone chimney is an unusual rock formation called Chimney Rock. It rises about 500' above the North Platte River. Why was Chimney Rock important to the early pioneers?
(answer: It was a landmark on the Oregon Trail that pioneers looked for to guide them on their way West; near Bayard)

WHO SAID THAT?

"There's no such thing as a bad boy," was what Edward Flanagan, a Catholic priest, said when he founded Boys Town in 1917. Boys Town is a home and school for neglected, abandoned, or underprivileged boys and girls. Just think of all the boys and girls (since 1979) that this American tradition has helped.

LIGHTS, CAMERA, ACTION!

Make a movie in your mind. This one stars Abraham *Lincoln*, our 16th President, as a statue. What's different about this statue? Lincoln's *knees* are made of *brass*, and they're shiny. Knee + brass = Nebraska. And what's the capital of Nebraska? Our 16th President, Lincoln. Lincoln, Nebraska.

"GO BIG RED!"

Bumper stickers, car decals, T-shirts, and caps that say, "Go Big Red," tell the story about Nebraskans' interest in football. The "Big Red" are the University of Nebraska's Cornhuskers, and every fall, over 70,000 sports enthusiasts pack Memorial Stadium in Lincoln to cheer for their Big Eight team. Why do you think the Cornhuskers are called the "Big Red"?

NEBRASKA

JUST IMAGINE

The weary horses and cattle are corralled for the night and they graze on the tall grass. The wagons are arranged in a circle for protection even though Indian attacks are rare. A central fire is blazing and lanterns flicker under the canvas of the wagons as you see silhouettes of children grabbing feather pillows and quilts, and settling down for the night. The warmth of the wagons looks cozy against a dark, starry night sky. Some of the men are sitting around the campfire talking about how one of the wagons lost a wheel as the eight-yoked oxen swam across the Platte River, "Lucky that extra wheels are carried. Will we ever reach Utah?" Just imagine leaving your home, packing only your most prized possessions, and traveling hundreds of miles in a covered wagon. Can you imagine?

WHO SAID THAT?

The "Great Migration" starting in 1843 saw over half a million pioneers walking, pulling handcarts, riding horseback, and driving covered wagons, across Nebraska, heading West. The Oregon Trail, the Mormon Trail, and the Lewis and Clark Trail became famous routes for those looking for land and riches. To migrate means to go from one region to settle in another.

WHEN IS A CAPITAL A CAPITOL?

Only when it's a building. To help you remember which spelling is correct, here's a hint that may help. The name of the location or the city is spelled "capital." If you're talking about the building itself, as in the capitol building, it's spelled "capitol." Think of the "O" in capitol as the dome that sits on top of the capitol building. Most capitol buildings have an O-shaped dome on top, like our U.S. capitol building in Washington, D.C. or maybe your own state capitol building. You will now always know that the building (with the dome letter "O") is spelled c-a-p-i-t-o-l. Can you remember the difference?

CRISPY CRACKERS

With all the different grains grown in Nebraska, it's time to celebrate our agricultural past.

Here's what you need:

1 cup whole wheat flour
¼ tsp. salt
½ tsp. baking powder
cream

Here's what you do:

Combine flour, salt, and baking powder and sift into bowl. Add enough cream so everything sticks together and the dough can be rolled out on a floured board or counter top. Roll out thin and cut into cracker-size shapes, or whatever shape you'd like. Be creative! Bake on a lightly greased cookie sheet at 400° until brown. If you want them crispier, reheat the crackers after they've been baked once and have cooled. Where's the jam?

A Tea Party? . . .No, it's a TREE party!

With Nebraska the home of Arbor Day, you might ask yourself how your neighborhood or school is fixed for trees? Get some friends together and visit a local nursery. Ask if they'll donate some little tree seedlings for your school, church, or neighborhood. Explain that you're interested in "greening up" sites in your city. Can you tell them why? (Consider shelter for animals, cleaning up the air, stopping erosion.) Most nurseries will be agreeable. Don't forget to say "thank you" and then plan your TREE party. Have fun with this and serve only foods that have the word or sound of "tree" in them, such as pastry (pas-tree), poultry (poul-tree), and if you're really stuck, you can always serve any treat (tree-t)!

NORTH DAKOTA

The deep red-rose wild prairie rose with its yellow center is the state flower. How about choosing a deep rosy red for North Dakota on your America! map?

©owboys used to sing about the Red River Valley for good reason. It's one of the most beautiful and fertile valleys in all America. With its rich topsoil, farmers all agree on one thing: If it can't grow in the Red River Valley, it won't grow anywhere! The *Flickertail State*, named for a ground squirrel, is located in the exact middle of North America. It has an amazing landscape of grassy plains, stony ridges, gorges, buttes, and the rugged Badlands. Amazing, too, are those hearty North Dakotans who still have that pioneering spirit!

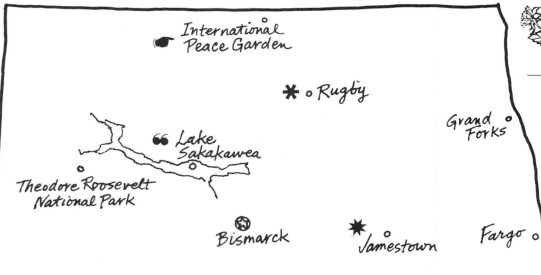

International Peace Garden

✱ ○ Rugby

Grand Forks ○

❝❞ Lake Sakakawea

Theodore Roosevelt National Park

Bismarck

✱ Jamestown ○

Fargo ○

PICTURE THIS

North Dakota looks like a rectangle with an uneven eastern border. The northeast corner leans toward the west.

DID YOU KNOW?

The Theodore Roosevelt National Park is the only national park created in memory of a single person.

WHICH DAKOTA CAME FIRST?

North Dakota and South Dakota became states on the same day November 2, 1889, but no one will ever know which state became a state first. When President Benjamin Harrison was signing the documents, he shuffled the papers several times and then covered the top half of the document, so he wouldn't know which one he was signing. The two states are now ranked in alphabetical order with North Dakota as the 39th state, and South Dakota as the 40th. Do you think President Harrison's idea was a good one?

THE CURIOUS W's

Who? From my experiences of frontier life, I wrote western novels. In fact, I wrote hundreds of stories about survival in the Old West. For my work I received the Presidential Medal of Freedom in 1984. Who am I?
(answer: Louis L'Amour; Jamestown)

What? A tower looms above the landscape in the Turtle Mountains. The site was donated by the Canadian province of Manitoba and North Dakota. The only one of its kind in the world, it celebrates the many years of peace between the U.S. and Canada. What is this?
(answer: The International Peace Garden; north of Dunseith)

Where? The city's name is Rugby, and it's 1,500 miles from the Pacific Ocean, 1,500 miles from the Atlantic Ocean, and the same distance from the Gulf of Mexico and the Arctic Ocean. Where in the U.S.A. is Rugby, the geographic center of the North American continent?

Why? Lake Sakakawea is named for Lewis and Clark's Shoshone Indian guide, Sakakawea (or Sakajawea). The lake is a reservoir behind a dam that holds back the waters of the mighty Missouri River. Why is this lake unique?
(answer: It is the largest man-made lake in the U.S.A., located entirely within one state.)

Make a movie in your mind. Picture a man at the *North* Pole wearing a *coat* and throwing snowballs at walruses. He's *missed* the *mark*, and hit a polar bear on the nose. Look out! Here comes the polar bear. North + coat = North Dakota and missing the mark = Bismarck, capital. Bismarck, North Dakota.

GO FOR THE GOLD!

Stage your own family, school, class, or neighborhood Olympics. Invent your own events and make medals for awards. Cut cardboard circles and paint them gold (first place), silver (second place), and bronze (third place). Glue or staple a length of ribbon to the back so it will fit over a head. Use your imagination and hunt around for stickers, beads, and other trinkets that would make your medals one-of-a-kind.

Events? Running, skipping, hopping races; obstacle course; ball throws; basketball shooting; ball toss into a bucket; balance beam on the ground (2" x 4" plus length to walk). You decide. You could even make three victory stands out of stools, sturdy boxes, or crates. What a great idea for an all-American birthday party right in your own backyard!

Have you ever heard the saying, "Water, water everywhere but not a drop to drink."? Guess how many gallons of drinking water can be polluted by one gallon of motor oil leaking into the ground . . . 2,500 gallons, 25,000 gallons, 250,000 gallons? Would you believe 250,000 gallons! Don't be a water polluter.

PACK YOUR BAGS

The Olympic Games in North Dakota? Athletes come from all over the state to participate in the newly organized Prairie Rose State Games. They're a miniature Olympics for amateurs, and the games feature track and field events, bicycling, and most of the "real" Olympic events.

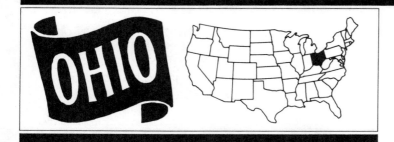

The Iroquois called it "Oheo," and to them it meant something beautiful or the great river. To Ohioans today, it still has the same meaning. Land and water are vital to the Buckeye State's manufacturing and industry, with Lake Erie in the north, and the vast Ohio River connecting to other waterways. Between large, populated cities lie vast farmlands and small towns. The Iroquois were right —"Oheo" is beautiful.

With the scarlet carnation as the state flower, tomato juice as the state drink, the ladybug as the state insect, what color do you suppose the state bird is? If you're thinking "red," you're right! It's the cardinal, and what about the Cincinnati Reds and the Cleveland Indians? With red such a prominent state color, what else could Ohio be on your America! map?

PICTURE THIS

The shape of Ohio looks like the outline of a shield, just like the knights of old carried. Imagine yourself painting one of these shields. The paint is wet, is dripping southward. Can you see the shield losing its shape and the paint dripping off?

THE CURIOUS W's

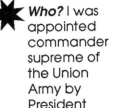 **Who?** I was appointed commander supreme of the Union Army by President Lincoln, and I was the commanding general who received Robert E. Lee's surrender of the  Confederate Army at the end of the Civil War. Some said the U.S. in my name stood for "United States," while others thought it stood for "Uncle Sam" or "Unconditional Surrender." Who am I?
(answer: Ulysses S. Grant; Point Pleasant)

What? A statue of Jim Thorpe stands in front of this popular complex. Thorpe played football for the Canton Bulldogs and, today, the best professional football players of all time are honored at this site. What is it?
(answer: Pro Football Hall of Fame; Canton)

Why? The city of Akron has meant something to young people from all over the country. This famous event takes place in August, and this is one race where the announcer doesn't have to say, "Gentlemen, start your engines." There are no engines! Why is Akron well-known to many young people?
(answer: It hosts the annual All-American Soap Box Derby; Akron)

 Make a movie in your mind and see someone waving his hand high into the air and calling out, "*Oh, Hi!*" Who is this person? It's Christopher *Columbus*! He's just landed miles off his course. "Oh" + "Hi" = Ohio, and Columbus = Columbus, Ohio's capital. Columbus, Ohio.

TRUTH TAKES A STAND

With men booing and shouting at her, the mother of 13 children stepped up to the microphone at a women's rights convention. The year was 1851 and the place was Akron, Ohio. She courageously gave a speech about the poor treatment of blacks and women. She knew what to say because she was born a slave in Ulster County, New York, and even when slavery was abolished, she was still held against her will. Once she had escaped, she changed her name to Sojourner Truth. She spent the rest of her life working for human rights.

CATCHACLUE

  Oberlin College in Ohio has the unique distinction among men and women of America of being the first college to be
(a) a dental school
(b) a coeducational school
(c) a night school.
(answer: (b); clue: men and women = coeducational)

HIP, HIP, HOORAY!

He loved to plant trees and seeds and seedlings, and before he was done, he planted hundreds and hundreds of acres of trees in the great Ohio Valley. His name was John Chapman, and he especially liked to plant apple seeds, so he earned the appropriate nickname of Johnny Appleseed. What a great American naturalist, conservationist, and folk hero!

SOUTH DAKOTA

COLOR AMERICA!

Springtime is when South Dakota's wildflowers, with names like shooting stars, baby's breath, fleur-de-lis, and wood orchids, color the hills and plains. The first flower of spring, the lavender-colored pasqueflower, is the state flower. How about coloring South Dakota the pale purple of the pasqueflower?

The *Coyote State* has been a challenge to the early Indians, pioneers, settlers, and farmers. Battling the extremes of heat and cold, rugged terrain, and blizzards on the wind-swept high plains, South Dakotans are survivors and builders. Divided by the great Missouri River, the state echoes with unmatched prehistoric fossil beds, Wild West legends, a gold rush, fur traders and forts, buffalo herds, and homesteaders. Home to the Badlands and Black Hills, South Dakota is a kaleidoscope of natural wonders and history.

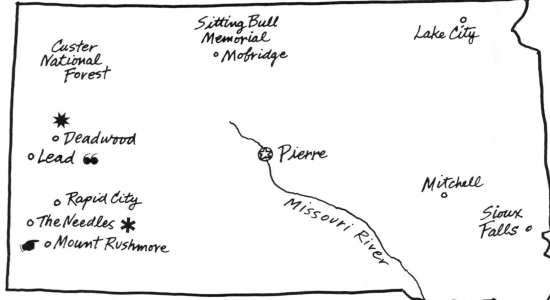

Sitting Bull Memorial
Lake City
Custer National Forest
o Mobridge
Deadwood
o Lead 👀
⊛ Pierre
Mitchell
o Rapid City
The Needles ✳
Sioux Falls o
o Mount Rushmore
Missouri River

PACK YOUR BAGS

Wind blowing in and out of the cave is how Wind Cave National Park got its name. Underground are beautiful limestone crystal formations that look even more spectacular during a candle light tour. This is America's first cave national park and one of the largest caverns in the world.

ARE THE BLACK HILLS REALLY BLACK?

They probably got their name years ago because of the thick forests which made them look dark from a distance. The Black Hills are really high ridges, jagged peaks, crags, valleys, and forests.

PICTURE THIS

South Dakota looks like a rectangle with some of the rectangle bulging out of the southeast corner and a bite missing in the northeast.

Who? I was a U.S. marshal, fast with a gun, and I cleared many a frontier town of outlaws. I was killed playing poker, and I'm buried in Deadwood near Calamity Jane, the famous frontierswoman. Who am I?
(answer: James Butler "Wild Bill" Hickock; Deadwood)

What? It took 14 years of measuring, drilling, blasting, splitting, and smoothing to form the gigantic heads of Presidents Washington, Jefferson, Teddy Roosevelt, and Lincoln. Gutzon Borglum was the designer and sculptor, but experienced miners did much of the cutting and blasting of the granite. What is this historical site?

(answer: Mount Rushmore; near Rapid City)

Where? Strange needle-like granite spires look like huge spears jutting up into the sky. They were formed millions of years ago by water and wind erosion. One of the spires has an "eye" in it that makes it look very much like a gigantic needle. Where is the Needles Highway?
(answer: Black Hills region)

Why? The Homestake Mine at Lead (rhymes with Feed) with its hundreds of miles of tunnels is a mile high, but that's not its claim to fame. Why is the Homestake Mine of Gold Run Gulch a winner?
(answer: It has produced more gold than any other single mine in the world.)

LIGHTS, CAMERA, ACTION!

Make a movie in your mind. Pictu[re the] Missouri River and the *sun* is beati[ng on] the ship. He gets so hot that he tak[es] it on *Pier E* where the ship is docke[d...] Dakota, and Pier E = Pierre. Now yo[u...] South Dakota.

120

HOME-GROWN PRIMEVAL FOREST

You can easily create your own prehistoric fern garden. It grows quickly, and if you'd like to make it look like a miniature of the real thing, *here's what you need:* An old, shallow baking pan, sand, garden soil, several fresh carrots. *Here's what you do:*

1. Place some sand in the bottom of the pan, then the garden soil — about half full will do.

2. Cut away all of the carrot except about half an inch of the thick end at the top.

3. Put several carrot tops into the soil, pressing the soil around each one, but do not cover the tops.

4. Sprinkle lightly with water. When your fern forest starts to grow, how about adding some little plastic dinosaur figures and a few stones and pebbles?

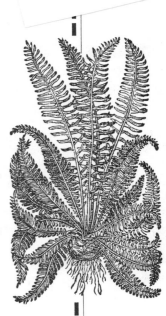

HIP, HIP, HOORAY!

Sioux Indian Chief Henry Standing Bear told his people that he thought the Native Americans should have a statue like the white men had at Mount Rushmore. The Sioux Council selected a sculpture that shows Chief Crazy Horse riding a snorting horse. When completed, it will be the largest in the world - an enormous 400' long and 500' high! The artist, Korczak Ziolkowski, died before he could complete the work, but his family is pursuing its completion.

WISCONSIN

"Say cheese!" and you'll know what color to make Wisconsin on your America! map. How about a deep orange color of sharp cheddar, or maybe a lighter color for Wisconsin's very own colby? Since Wisconsin is "America's Dairyland," the color of your favorite ice cream flavor would look tempting, too. Yum!

A "good place to live" is what the Menominee Indians meant when they said, "wee-schoseck," and most Wisconsinites will nod their heads "Yes" to that. Touched by Lakes Superior and Michigan, this "Land of Lakes" has an unbelievable amount of fresh water with over 15,000 lakes. The state, with its capital named for a president, is a pastoral treasure.

Conservation Conscious Wisconsin

What happened to all of the beautiful trees? Years ago when lumber was needed for building and making paper products, many of Wisconsin's forests were cut down. In fact, entire forests were destroyed. Today, Wisconsin lumber and paper companies are planting more trees than they're cutting down. Many wilderness areas are now protected, and wildlife is flourishing because Wisconsin cares.

Map

LAKE SUPERIOR

Copper Falls State Park

Eau Claire

Wisconsin River

Wausau

Green Bay

Oshkosh

Wisconsin Dells

Baraboo Circus World

Milwaukee

Spring Green

Madison

LAKE MICHIGAN

PICTURE THIS

Wisconsin looks like a boxing glove. Can you see the thumb of the glove sticking out toward the east into Lake Michigan? The top of the glove seems to be punching to the north and hitting Lake Superior.

THE CURIOUS W's

Who? We started out by putting on little shows with rabbits, chickens, a goat, and a horse, and a few other farm animals. After awhile we added some tents, and before long we had started our own circus. It became the largest circus in the world. Who are we?
(answer: The Ringling brothers, whose circus became Ringling Brothers and Barnum and Bailey Circus; Baraboo)

What? Frank Lloyd Wright is one of America's cherished architects. He designed spectacular buildings and homes. He designed his own summer home which is now a school. What is its name?
(answer: Taliesin; Spring Green)

Where? The Wisconsin River has turned this seven-mile stretch of sandstone rock along its shores into unusually formed gorges and canyons. Thousands of visitors a year ride in amphibious trucks called "ducks" that drive into the river for the floating tour. Where is Wisconsin Dells?

Why? Oshkosh is a label we see on clothing, but why is this city known throughout the world to aviation buffs?
(answer: The Oshkosh Fly-in takes place in July and thousands of planes fly-in for a world class exhibit of every kind of plane imaginable; Oshkosh)

LIGHTS, CAMERA, ACTION! Make a movie in your mind. Imagine you are making a *wish* at your birthday party. You look up into the sky and see the sun, and boy, is the sun mad! The *mad sun* didn't get a piece of birthday cake, so he melted all of the ice cream. Uh-oh! Wish = Wisconsin, and a mad sun = Madison, its capital. Madison, Wisconsin.

DID YOU KNoW? Many of our country's Native Americans live on reservations, and these reservations are like separate states. The residents make their own laws and enforce them. While on the reservation, the laws of the state do not apply, but when a person leaves the boundaries of the reservation, then the state's laws must be obeyed. Over 800,000 Native Americans live on Indian reservations in the United States.

ⓒⒶⓉⒸⒽ Ⓐ ⓒⓁⓊⒺ

Many people are led to believe that the *Badger State* is nicknamed because of the many badgers in the state, but it really has to do with the nickname given to Wisconsin's
(a) lead miners
(b) Native Americans
(c) police department.
(answer: (a); clue: led = lead)

PACK YOUR BAGS Neighborhoods of Germans, African Americans, Scandinavians, Irish, Polish, and Serbian are close-knit and have had a great influence on Milwaukee's culture. The Germans introduced beer to the area after first arriving from Europe, and today Milwaukee is home to many of the nation's largest breweries. Baseball's American League team is named the Brewers. Isn't it interesting how people from other countries have played such an important part in America's culture from sea to shining sea?

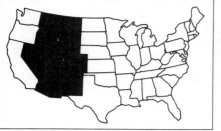

THE ROCKY MOUNTAIN STATES

NAME THE CAPITAL

How many capitals of the Rocky Mountain states can you name? Write the names below, then check your answers on the state maps. Each state capital is marked with a ✪. Did you get all eight state capitals correct?

ARIZONA _____

COLORADO _____

IDAHO _____

MONTANA _____

NEVADA _____

NEW MEXICO _____

UTAH _____

WYOMING _____

Arizona's year-round sunshine makes it one of our country's favorite places to visit and live. Over two million people a year stand hundreds of feet above the Colorado River and view the spectacular Grand Canyon, one of the seven natural wonders of the world. With 14 Indian tribes represented, Arizona has the largest Native American population of all the states. Thrilling legends of the Old West and a blending of Indian, Spanish, and Mexican cultures give the *Grand Canyon State* its matchless character and charm.

Stately saguaro cacti are found in just two of our states. Arizona has many other cactus varieties too, and most of them are in shades of green. A prickly cactus green would look great on Arizona.

Lake Powell

Grand Canyon

Colorado River

Flagstaff

Meteor Crater

Prescott National Forest

Phoenix

Gila River

Yuma

Organ Pipe Cactus National Monument

Tucson

Tombstone

Rain-less

A region with less than 10 inches of rain is called an arid region; with less than 15 inches it's called semi-arid. An example of an arid and semi-arid region is in the Great Basin of North America. Do you live in an arid or semi-arid region?

Picture This

Arizona looks like a broken chisel on the southwest corner, because there's no point. Also at the western edge it appears broken, because it is jagged.

How's your Latitude Attitude?

Are Phoenix, Arizona and Shikoku, Japan on the same approximate latitude (33°N) as Augusta, Georgia or Tulsa, Oklahoma?

THE CURIOUS W's

 **Who?** I was chief of the southern Chiricahua band of Apache Indians, and along with Cochise, we're the best known Apache chiefs. I resisted the white man's efforts to drive us from our lands, but after many years of brutal fighting, I finally surrendered. Who am I?
(answer: Geronimo, born in Arizona)

What? It's three miles around, nearly one mile across, and an astounding 570 feet deep. Scientists from all over the world have come to Arizona to take a look at this "hole." Its rim rises another 150 feet above the plain. What is this?
(answer: Meteor Crater, probably formed when 60,000 tons of iron and nickel hit the earth; 37 miles east of Flagstaff)

Where? Layer upon layer, color upon color, this vast, magnificent natural wonder is not only Arizona's and America's, but it is also a world treasure. Its layered walls can be read like a book. The colors and rocks tell a story that dates back to the beginning of our earth. This would have to be the Grand Canyon. Do you know where it is?

Why? Tombstone started out as a silver mining town, but ended up securing a place in our history because of an event that took place here between U.S. marshal Wyatt Earp, Doc Holliday, and the Clanton Gang. Do you know why Tombstone is a famous Old West site?
(answer: It was where the gunfight at the O.K. Corral took place, a celebrated shoot-out; Tombstone)

LIGHTS, CAMERA, ACTION! Make a movie in your mind. Picture the mythological bird, the phoenix, flying in the air, way up high near the ozone layer. Suddenly it can't breathe and the *phoenix* swoops lower to get into the *air zone*. The capital of Arizona is easy. Air + zone = Arizona and phoenix = Phoenix. Phoenix, Arizona

A cactus has really saved a life? Absolutely! Very likely, many people have survived the searing heat thanks to this desert friend. The rotund barrel cactus stores the most liquid of any cactus, and many desert travelers who were stranded, lost, or without sufficient water have cut into the barrel cactus to quench their thirst and even save a life. The saguaro cactus — the tall one with its "arms" pointing upward — can store four-fifths of its weight in water. It only opens up its pores at night to conserve the water. If you were without water in the desert, what plant would you look for?

The sun is so very important to the earth. It's our nearest star, only 93 million miles away. Believe it or not, it takes light from the sun only 8$\frac{1}{3}$ minutes to reach the earth. Do you remember the speed of light? That's right, light travels at 186,000 miles per second. Now that's fast!

PLANT A MINIATURE CACTUS GARDEN

You don't need to live in the desert to enjoy your own miniature cactus garden. In fact, cacti make very hardy indoor plants, and many people enjoy growing enormous cacti right in their homes. It's kind of fun to have a cactus growing in your room in the middle of a bitter cold winter. *Here's what you need*: potting soil; a few small varieties of cacti available at your garden center or florist (try to buy three different sizes and shapes); a shallow clay pot or bowl; some plant food; some interesting stones or rocks. *Here's what you do:*

1. Arrange your cacti in the soil, so that you balance out the shapes and sizes. Gently pack the soil around the roots. Arrange some decorative rocks or stones (you may want to paint them natural sand and sun colors) in the cactus dish.

2. Water your cacti generously right after you plant them. Then water them when the soil feels dry, but don't overwater. Keep your cactus in a sunny to partially sunny room. Some kinds actually do fine in a darker room, so check the directions that came with yours.

3. Feed your cactus with plant food every month.

PACK YOUR BAGS

Rodeos, gold panning, and imaginary gun fights give Arizona a taste of the Old West. White water rafting, skiing in both winter and summer, and yes, even dog sledding, add lots of variety to the entertainment found in the Grand Canyon State. A hair-raising helicopter ride right through the middle of the Grand Canyon offers a thrill a minute plus breath-taking, panoramic views.

DID YOU KNoW ?

How did the Petrified Forest get petrified? A large fresh water lake, 3,000 feet deep, covered the forested valley over 200 million years ago. The lake water came from rivers and streams, and with the water came dirt containing minerals. The water with the minerals seeped into the trees. When the lake waters eventually drained away, the minerals remained inside the tree trunks and hardened into stone. That's enough to petrify anything! Petrified wood looks like beautifully colored glass.

When the early Spanish explorers first looked at the great river, they called it the Colorado, because its churning waters carried silt (soil) that gave the water a reddish tint. Since Colorado means "colored red" in Spanish, how about a little colorado on your America! map?

Colorado has 54 mountains with altitudes over 14,000 feet, more than any other state. The rugged Rocky Mountains soar above Colorado, and Denver is our nation's only "Mile High" capital. The Rockies are the youngest major mountain range in the world — only babies at 60 million years old. Along with the mountains, Colorado has beautiful flat plains for agriculture, too. With a shiny twenty-four-carat gold dome on its capitol, Coloradans are reminded of its gold rush days. Colorado has its gold, but its real wealth lies in its breath-taking beauty.

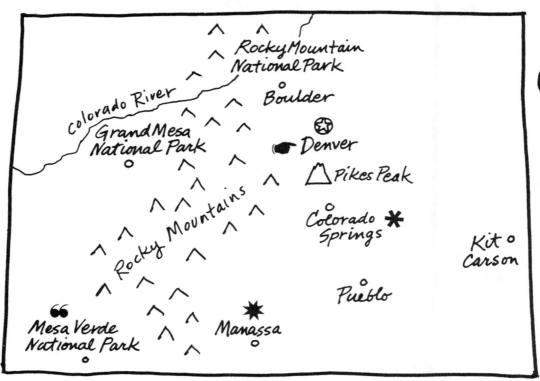

PICTURE THIS

Colorado is almost a perfect rectangle, bowed slightly at the top.

Isn't it remarkable that in a state which has more than 1,000 mountain peaks over 10,000 feet tall, there are also some of the largest sand dunes in our country? Some of these towering hills of glistening white sand reach heights of over 600 feet!

DID YOU KNOW?

THE CURIOUS W's

Who? I was nicknamed the "Manassa Mauler" because I was born in Manassa, and I'm a boxer. In fact, I was the world heavyweight boxing champion in 1919. When I worked in mining camps, I started boxing, but I didn't know at the time that I'd become one of the best-known heavyweight fighters of all time. Who am I?
(answer: Jack Dempsey; Manassa)

What? Some of the stuff that jingles in your pocket was probably made here. Over five billion coins are made here a year. Our paper money is made at the Bureau of Printing and Engraving in Washington, D.C. What is this "coin only" place called in Colorado?
(answer: The Denver Mint; Denver)

Where? "O beautiful, for spacious skies, for amber waves of grain . . ." are words that most Americans sing in a favorite patriotic song. These words were written by Katherine Lee Bates at the top of Colorado's most famous peak. Do you know its name and where it's located?
(Pikes Peak; near Colorado Springs)

Why? The early residents of this site were basket makers, and many years later, the people built round pit houses that were like basements with high walls with roofs made out of logs held together with mud. Mesa Verde National Park holds a unique distinction. Why?
(answer: largest site of ancient Indian cliff dwellings in the world; near Cortez)

LIGHTS, CAMERA, ACTION!
Make a movie in your mind. Picture that you have just painted your *den* a bright *color* of *red*. Ooops, you've made a mistake. It had wallpaper made of *fur*, and all the fur has turned to red. The capital of Colorado is yours. Color + red = Colorado, and den + fur = Denver. Denver, Colorado.

C A T C H A C L U E

The Colorado River drains about one-twelfth of the U.S. This is a large part of the nation. The Colorado River is
(a) the largest river west of the Rockies
(b) the continental divide
(c) the annual snow pack of the Rocky Mountains.
(answer: (a); clue: large = largest)

P·A·R·K·S & "P·A·R·K·S"
When is a park not a grassy picnic area with swings, trees, paths, and maybe a lake? It's when it's in Colorado, and it's a "park," the name given to a very high altitude valley between Colorado's towering mountain ranges. Many of these "park" areas are huge. One is larger than the whole state of Connecticut!

COLORADO

The *Continental Divide*: If you make a mountain by leaning two cards together, so they form "A," which way would the water flow? The continental divide can be pictured the same way. Water falling on the east side of the Rockies flows into the Gulf of Mexico. The water falling on the west side of the Rockies flows into the Pacific Ocean. The Continental Divide is along the Rocky Mountains and is also known as the watershed of North America.

WHAT'S IN A (NICK)NAME?

Nicknames usually reveal something about someone or something. Usually if you know the person or thing, the reason for the nickname becomes pretty clear, right? So why is Colorado's nickname, the *Centennial State*? Centennial means 100th birthday or anniversary. Colorado joined the Union in 1876, on the 100th anniversary, or centennial, of the signing of the Declaration of Independence in 1776. Pretty clever nickname!

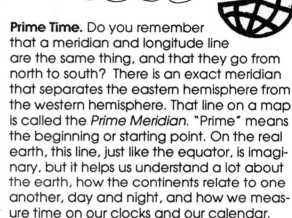

Prime Time. Do you remember that a meridian and longitude line are the same thing, and that they go from north to south? There is an exact meridian that separates the eastern hemisphere from the western hemisphere. That line on a map is called the *Prime Meridian*. "Prime" means the beginning or starting point. On the real earth, this line, just like the equator, is imaginary, but it helps us understand a lot about the earth, how the continents relate to one another, day and night, and how we measure time on our clocks and our calendar.

This imaginary line goes through Greenwich, England starting at the North Pole and ending at the South Pole (curved just like the letter "C"). If you go west or left from the Prime Meridian, and keep going west until you are half way around the earth, you will have "traveled" past 180 meridians. (Meridians are measured in degrees.) The meridian where the lines coming from the west and the lines coming from the east meet is called the *International Date Line*, where supposedly every calendar date begins. It is on the 180° meridian. If you look at a globe or in an atlas at a world map that shows the earth's curvature, this will all become very clear to you. Want to cement it in your brain? Try drawing it!

What do people do 1,200 feet underground beneath Cheyenne Mountain near Colorado Springs? Are they mining or exploring caves? While America sleeps, NORAD (North American Aerospace Defense Command operations center) is tracking any moving man-made object in space from high-flying jets to satellites. It can also detect any possible missile attacks. Thank you, NORAD, for helping keep America safe.

PACK YOUR BAGS

Take your pick in Colorado. You can grab a "pick" and look for gold like the Fifty-Niners did during a brief gold rush, you can ski at over 30 areas such as the famous Aspen, Vail, and Snowmass resorts in winter, or try hiking the new Colorado Trail which takes backpackers across five major rivers and through seven national forests in the summertime.

SING OUT AMERICA

The history and beauty of many states and cities have caused people to write songs about them. You have probably heard John Denver's song, "Rocky Mountain High." And what about "New York! New York" and "I Left My Heart In San Francisco." Well, here's your chance to sing out.

Make up your own words about a famous American or state or city to familiar tunes such as "Jingle Bells," "Did You Ever See A Lassie," "Row, Row, Row Your Boat," or "When The Saints Come Marching In." For example, to the tune of "Old MacDonald":

Old Ben Franklin flew a kite
On a stormy night,
And on his kite he had a key
On a stormy night.
With a spark, spark, here,
And a spark spark there...

Idaho has its famous potatoes, but guess what else? The *Gem State* is the nation's leading producer of silver, and its state gem is the star garnet. Star garnets are mined in Idaho for commercial use. When they are polished, they are a deep, deep red in color, and they seem to sparkle like little stars. Would this deep red be a good color for your America! map?

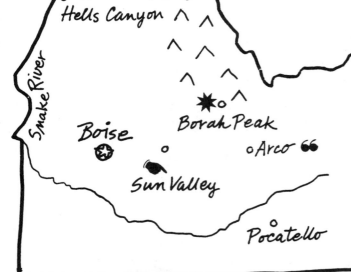

Whether you're eating French fried, baked, mashed, or hash browns, chances are you're eating a famous Idaho potato. Idaho is also famous for its surging, cascading rivers. White water rafting fans will tell you that the Salmon and Snake rivers have some of the most thrilling and challenging white water rapids in the nation — some so treacherous that only the most experienced guides will take on the mighty, churning runs. Idaho, with its spectacular beauty, was called "ee-da-how" by the Shoshone Indians, which means "see the sun coming down the mountain." Watching the sun set behind Idaho's mountainous backdrop, the Shoshone name is a good one for this state of natural wonders.

 **PICTURE THIS**

Doesn't Idaho look like a king's throne facing to the East? Do you have a chair shaped like that in your house?

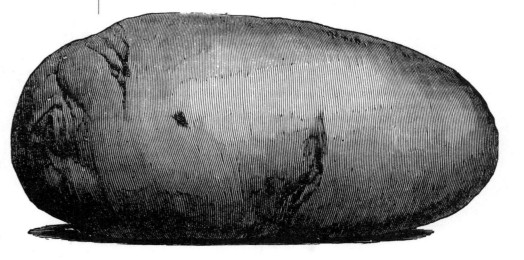

THE CURIOUS W's

 Who? Not many people can boast about having a mountain peak named after them, but I can, and it's the highest peak in Idaho. I served as a U.S. Senator for 33 years, and I'm proud of being responsible for the establishment of the U.S. Department of Labor. Name Idaho's highest peak and you'll know my name.
(William Borah, born in Illinois, but spent most of his life in Idaho. Can you find Borah Peak?)

What? Winter or summer, this famous resort tops the list of tourism in Idaho. It offers some of the best downhill and cross-country skiing in the U.S. Trail trips on horseback during the summertime are also popular at this favorite recreational site. What is its name?
(answer: Sun Valley; east of Boise)

Where? If you've ever been to the Grand Canyon, or if you've seen pictures of it, you'll be struck by how deep it is. But when you see Hell's Canyon on the Idaho-Oregon border, you'll be amazed to know that it is much deeper than the Grand Canyon. In fact, some of its steep walls rise over 9,000 feet above the churning rapids of the Snake River. Can you find Hell's Canyon, the deepest canyon in North America?

Why? This National Historic Landmark is not in operation, but you can visit this site to get a glimpse of an important milestone in America's energy production. Called the Experimental Breeder Reactor #1, can you take a guess why this power plant was important?
(answer: It was the first atomic power plant in the world to produce electricity; near Arco)

 Make a movie in your mind. Picture a lot of boys looking down on a potato farm. What do the *boys see*? They see a girl named *Ida*, and what is Ida doing? Ida's hoeing those potatoes. The capital of Idaho is easy to remember. Boys + see = Boise and Ida + hoe = Idaho. Boise, Idaho.

 ⒸⒶⓉⒸⒽ Ⓐ ⒸⓁⓊⒺ

 Lewiston, Idaho is a few hundred miles from the Pacific Ocean. With this fact in mind, you will be surprised to find that Lewiston has
(a) the largest salmon cannery in the western U.S.
(b) a salt conversion center
(c) a Pacific Ocean port.
(answer: (c); clue: Pacific = Pacific)

 How's Your Latitude Attitude?

Are Boise, Idaho and Oshawa, Canada on the same approximate latitude (43°N) as Des Moines, Iowa or Concord, New Hampshire?

IDAHO

HIP, HIP, HOORAY!

Kids love to write on blackboards at school, and when Philo T. Farnsworth was 16 years old, he sketched something on the blackboard in his chemistry classroom at Rigby Senior High School. It looked interesting enough, even then, and many years later it made a great deal of sense. He sketched what he called an "image dissector tube" on the school blackboard. Today, the sign posted just outside of Rigby reads, "Welcome to Rigby— Birthplace of T.V." Philo T. Farnsworth, as an adult, invented the tube which we now call television. Millions of people throughout the world say, "Thank you, Philo."

PACK YOUR BAGS

Craters of the Moon National Monument are out of this world. Volcanic lava has shaped caves and tubes, cones, and lava fields, as far as you can see. Step on the cinder, and you'll think you're taking a moon walk. Camping, hiking, and biking at its best are only minutes away from Idaho's cities, so don't forget your inner tube or raft. With over 2,000 lakes and quiet streams for splashing and wading, to jet boats on the big rivers, Idaho is an enormous playground.

DID YOU KNOW ?

There are more Basques living in Idaho than in any other place outside of northern Spain. The northern mountain region of Spain is called the Basque region, and Basque people were originally sheep herders. When many of these people came to America, they settled in Idaho and became sheep herders here also. Idaho is proud of its Basque culture.

IDAHO POTATO ART

Even if you don't live in Idaho, potatoes are usually hiding out somewhere in your kitchen. Potatoes are excellent print-makers, and what could be more impressive than having your own personalized potato initial stamp?
Here's what you need: one potato, paring knife, tempera paint.

Here's what you do:

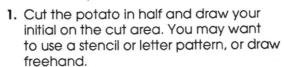

1. Cut the potato in half and draw your initial on the cut area. You may want to use a stencil or letter pattern, or draw freehand.

2. Use the paring knife to cut away the potato that surrounds your initial, including those hard to get to areas within a letter. When your initial looks like it's standing out from the rest of the potato, your potato print block is ready.

3. Dip your potato into a small, flat dish of the tempera paint and try it out on a piece of paper, until you get the right amount of paint . These initial prints will spiff up your book covers and binders for school, and you can even experiment with printing on cloth. Did someone say "wallpaper"? Now don't get carried away!

PACK YOUR BAGS

"If the people here trust you, they'll vote for you, even if they don't agree with you down the line," exclaimed Frank Church. Idahoans must have trusted him because he spent 24 years as their U.S. Senator. He's well-known for his conservation bills that have protected much of America's beautiful wilderness.

Butte, Montana is the center of an area that once supplied half of the copper for the U.S. Imagine a shiny new copper penny. Wouldn't that be a wonderful color for Montana on your America! map? You can try to capture that color by mixing brown and bright yellow crayons.

The *Treasure State* is Montana's official nickname, but it is also affectionately called "Big Sky Country" and the "Land of the Shining Mountains." Our fourth largest state in area is still filled with the wide open spaces of the early West. The Great Plains are high plains that stretch toward the awe-inspiring Rocky Mountains. Bighorn sheep, grizzly bear, buffalo, moose, and elk are found near the state's northern border of Canada, and Montana is the only contiguous state where wild wolf packs are still free to roam the immense, untouched wilderness.

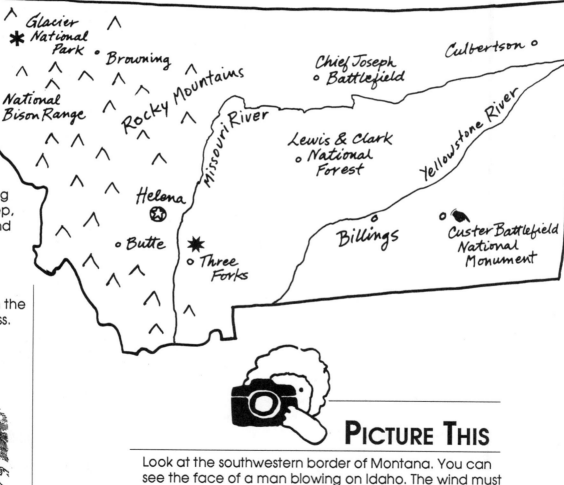

PICTURE THIS

Look at the southwestern border of Montana. You can see the face of a man blowing on Idaho. The wind must be coming from Canada which is above Montana. The man's hair is blowing straight back.

DID YOU KNOW?

The Missouri River has its source in Montana where the Madison, Jefferson, and Gallatin rivers meet between the towns of Logan and Three Forks. The peculiar thing about this is that the Missouri River then flows NORTH. The river then makes a large arc and turns east before it finally turns south. Even more interesting is that the Mississippi River does the exact same thing: North - East - South. Check it out.

THE CURIOUS W's

 Who? It took them over a month to get around the roaring waters of the Great Falls of the Missouri, but once they did, they crossed the Continental Divide and were on their way to the Pacific. The team explored many areas of Montana and found and named the source of the Missouri River. Their expedition paved the way for trappers and settlers. Who are they?
(answer: Meriwether Lewis and William Clark; source of the Missouri between Logan and Three Forks)

 What? Only one horse on the losing side was alive at the end of the most famous battle in history between the warriors of the Sioux and Cheyenne indians and U.S. cavalry troops. The Little Big Horn River was the 1876 site of this fierce stand off. What is the common name of this battle?
(answer: Custer's Last Stand; Little Big Horn River area, south of Hardin)

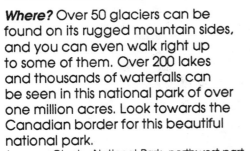

Where? Over 50 glaciers can be found on its rugged mountain sides, and you can even walk right up to some of them. Over 200 lakes and thousands of waterfalls can be seen in this national park of over one million acres. Look towards the Canadian border for this beautiful national park.
(answer: Glacier National Park; northwest part of the state)

Why? If you're up on your dinosaurs, you'll know why Hell Creek is a site that dinosaur lovers really dig. Why is Hell Creek of great interest?
(answer: A nearly complete tyrannosaurus rex skeleton was found here; Hell Creek, north of Jordan)

LIGHTS, CAMERA, ACTION! Make a movie in your mind. Picture a tall *mountain*. Who's on that mountain? It's a girl named Helen, and she's stuck on top of the mountain. Give *Helen a* hand and help her down. It's easy to see that mountain = Montana, and Helen + a = Helena. Helena, Montana. Easy, isn't it?

PACK YOUR BAGS

Camping, hiking, and fishing under Montana's big blue sky are a nature lover's dream come true. Or, what about putting on the old cowboy hat and going to a rodeo? Nearly every town in the state has a rodeo at some time during the year. Cold weather means snowshoeing, snowmobiling, and skiing, and Montana's got plenty of the white stuff in winter. Miles of snow-mobile runs and downhill and cross-country ski areas make winter sports exhilarating and fun in Montana. Why not try them all?

HIP, HIP, HOORAY!

When Jeannette Rankin took her place in the chamber of the U.S. House of Representatives, she was assured a place in America's history. In 1916 she became the first woman ever to be elected to the United States Congress.

MONTANA

STATE CONCENTRATION

Here's what you need: 100 pieces of paper, half with the name of the states on them, half with the names of the capitals.

Here's what you do: Shuffle the papers and spread them all out face down. Each person takes a turn by turning over any two cards. If the capital matches the state and the person *knows* that it is a match, the person keeps both cards. If they don't match or if the player doesn't recognize the match, turn the cards over in the same spot, and move on to the next player. Concentrate on the cards' locations. The player who ends up with the most matching cards is the winner.

Montana   Helena

·**And Just Where Was Sitting Bull?**·

Not at the Battle of Little Bighorn like many people think. In fact, Sitting Bull was not the chief of the Sioux. He was the tribe's medicine man! After the famous battle, he said that he wasn't surprised that Long Hair (Custer) and his soldiers lost, because they were tired and couldn't fire their rifles fast enough to ward off the Indian attack. He also said that Long Hair was a great "chief"!

The beautiful mountain bluebird is Nevada's state bird. Find the prettiest shade of feather blue for Nevada on your America! map. Blue and silver are the state's colors. Maybe you'd like to color Nevada silver instead... or how about stripes?

The gambling and entertainment capital of the United States title is claimed by Nevada. Big name performers and stars make Las Vegas and Reno light up every night of the year with musical extravaganzas and shows. But Nevada is far more than show biz. Its desert beauty unfolds as coyotes, foxes, badgers, rabbits, and an array of small desert creatures appear nightly. Rodeos as well as pioneer and Old West festivals are on-going events celebrating Nevada's colorful past. Camel races in Virginia City, wild burro races in Beatty, and air races in Reno are some of the excitement of Nevada.

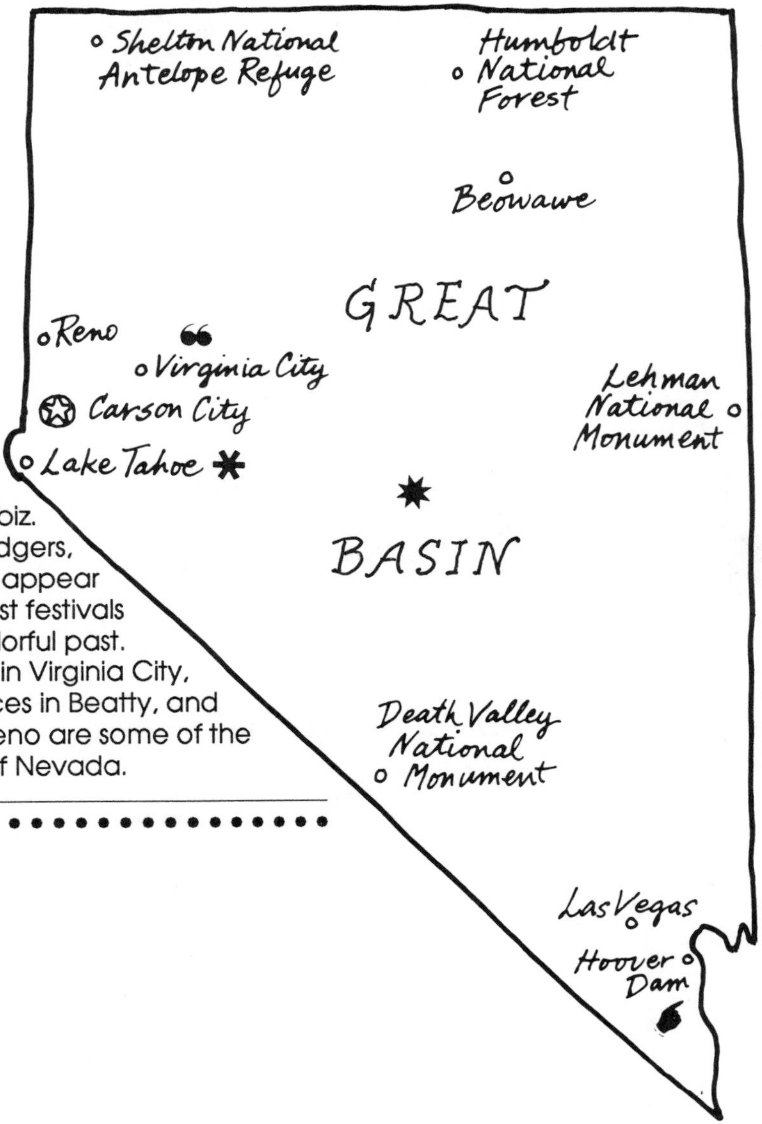

Shelton National Antelope Refuge

Humboldt National Forest

Beowawe

GREAT

Reno

Virginia City

Carson City

Lake Tahoe ✳

Lehman National Monument

BASIN

Death Valley National Monument

Las Vegas

Hoover Dam

HOW'S YOUR LATITUDE ATTITUDE?

Are Carson City, Nevada and Valencia, Spain on the same approximate latitude (39°N) as Dover, Delaware or Springfield, Missouri?

PICTURE THIS

During the French Revolution the peasants used guillotines to execute their condemned prisoners. Don't you think the shape of Nevada resembles this execution device? Look out California!

NEVADA

DID YOU KNoW ?

Nevada is the turquoise capital of the world. The bright blue-green semi-precious stone is used in making jewelry, especially the beautiful silver jewelry made by Native Americans. It is found in only a few places in the world. Can you believe that one chunk found in Nevada weighed over 150 pounds? That would make some necklace!

○ Turquoise and Silver Bracelets ○

Nevada is known for its beautiful turquoise and silver. Here's how to make a bracelet of your own.
Here's what you need: Aluminum foil, empty toilet tissue tube, small seashell macaroni, blue food coloring, white glue, scissors.
Here's what you do:

1. Cut the toilet tissue tube down one side. Cut out a section about 1¹/₂ " wide. Round off the edges to make a wide bracelet.

2. Cover it with a strip of aluminum foil, smoothing the edges on the inside of the bracelet.

3. Now, fill a cup with ¹/₂ cup water and several drops of blue food coloring. Drop in the macaroni shells and let set for about 10 minutes, until a bright blue. Remove and let dry.

4. When dry, glue turquoise "stones" onto the bracelet.

(From *Kids Create!* by Laurie Carlson, Williamson Publishing.)

Round off the edges of the tube section with scissors.

1¹/₂" wide

Lay the Tube section on the foil and wrap the foil around it.

Shiny side out

Foil

Tube section

Glue the turquoise "stones" in place.

=𝒲𝐸𝒜𝔱𝐡𝐸𝓡 𝐨𝓇 𝒩𝐨𝔱=

Which way do trade winds blow? Just remember the E at the end of the word trade and you will remember that trade winds blow from the east — from the northeast to the equator and from the southeast toward the equator or from NE to SW or from SE to NW. Look at a map to see if Nevada's weather is affected by the trade winds. What do you think?

THE CURIOUS W's

 Who? I've been called "The Pathfinder" because of the exploring and surveying I've done, especially in the West. I mapped Nevada for two years while traveling across the area with Kit Carson as my guide. Who am I?
(answer: John C. Frémont)

 What? Its concrete base is 660 feet thick, and the whole structure is made of enough concrete to pave a 16-foot wide highway from San Francisco to New York! It's located in Black Canyon, and it holds back the waters of the Colorado River. It's one of America's most powerful generators of electrical power. What is this famous dam?
(answer: Hoover Dam, south of Las Vegas on the Arizona-Nevada border)

 Where? This oval-shaped, deep blue lake is one of the deepest in the U.S. Sometimes the white caps and waves can get so rough during windy weather that they toss boats as if they're in an ocean. Beautiful homes and resorts line its shores, and it's a major Sierra Nevada recreation area. Where is Lake Tahoe?
(answer: on the California-Nevada border west of Carson City)

 Why? Henry T. Comstock said the "black stuff" and the "blue stuff" with the gold he'd found at Mount Davidson were "Worse'n useless." One prospector didn't believe him so he took some ore samples to an assay office in California. The discovery was named the Comstock Lode. Why was it important?
(answer: It's silver turned out to be worth more than the gold. It was a fabulous silver strike; Virginia City)

 Make a movie in your mind. Picture a *car* out in the *sun* with a *kitty* on top. The kitty is wearing flashy sunglasses, and singing and dancing, while waving to its fans. The kitty is in show biz in a big way. When you think of Nevada, think of show biz. Car + sun + kitty = Carson City. Carson City, Nevada. It's show time, ladies and gentlemen!

 PACK YOUR BAGS

Miles of sand and sagebrush stretch between many of Nevada's cities, and many of the fun things to do are in Reno and Las Vegas. Circus Circus in Las Vegas is like being under a real "big top" with trapeze artists gliding through the air and clowns and animals performing in the center ring. Spend a wonderful day visiting Hoover Dam where you can take an elevator ride into the depths of the dam and see how it works and how it was constructed. Afterwards, take a swim in Lake Mead, a most amazing manmade lake with its own beaches and marinas. There are all kinds of things to do in Nevada!

JUST IMAGINE

Have you ever wondered how some states get such strange nicknames? What would you have done if you were President Abraham Lincoln and you needed three more votes to pass a constitutional amendment? This amendment would do away with slavery. Where would you get the votes? Nevada was not a state at this time, so it couldn't vote. Guess what Lincoln did? He proposed that Nevada be admitted as a new state to the Union, and his plan worked. Nevada became a state, and Lincoln got the votes he needed. The year was 1864, and the rest of the United States was in the middle of the Civil War. *Battle Born State* is Nevada's nickname. Our 36th state was "born" during the Civil War!

CATCH A CLUE

 Take a chance and guess which state of the U.S. has the least rain of any state — usually under 7½ inches a year:
(a) Arizona
(b) Nevada
(c) New Mexico.
(answer: (b) Nevada; clue: chance (as in gambling) = Nevada)

NEW MEXICO

The beautiful blue-green color of turquoise is the color of New Mexico's state gem, which is the mineral, turquoise. Little specks of copper or iron give the stone a sparkling shimmer. Early New Mexico Indians used turquoise in jewelry-making, especially with silver to create some magnificent works of art. Turquoise would be a "gem" of a color on your America! map.

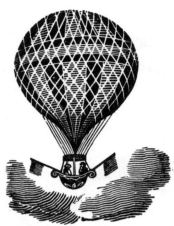

Parts of New Mexico are in ruins, and residents of the *Land of Enchantment* are proud of it! Extraordinary remnants of the past are found throughout this state of dramatic vistas. Many archaeologists believe that areas in New Mexico and the Southwest were the very first settlements in the Western Hemisphere. Fiestas, celebrations, and ceremonies pay tribute to New Mexico's Asian, Spanish, and American Indian past. Our nation's fifth largest state is a Southwest wonder.

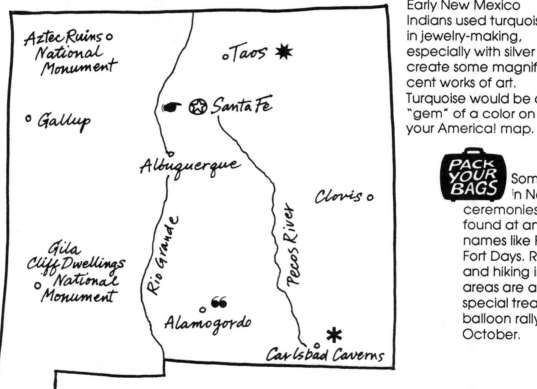

Aztec Ruins National Monument

Gallup

Santa Fe

Taos

Albuquerque

Clovis

Pecos River

Rio Grande

Gila Cliff Dwellings National Monument

Alamogordo

Carlsbad Caverns

PACK YOUR BAGS Something is always happening in New Mexico. Colorful Indian ceremonies and Mexican fiestas can be found at any time of the year with names like Fiesta de Santa Fe and Old Fort Days. Rock climbing, backpacking, and hiking in the rugged mountain areas are also popular pastimes. For a special treat, the world's largest hot air balloon rally is held in Albuquerque in October.

PICTURE THIS

New Mexico looks like a flag waving east toward Texas and Oklahoma, with its flagpole cut short. The bottom of the flagpole must be lost somewhere in Mexico.

THE CURIOUS W's

Who? I hitched up with a wagon train heading west when I was 17 years old, and I took care of the livestock for the fur traders. I became a well-known frontiersman, trapper, guide, and explorer before settling in Taos as the Indian agent for the Apache and Ute indians. My first name is Christopher, but you may know me by my nickname. Who am I?
(answer: Christopher "Kit" Carson; Taos)

What? Bandits and Indians on the war-path lay in wait for the wagon trains using this often dangerous route

from Independence, Missouri to Santa Fe. When conditions improved, over 5,000 wagon trains a year traveled the 800-mile route. What is this famous trail of the Old West?
(answer: The Santa Fe Trail)

Where? 700 feet down inside the earth you can see a limestone cavern which is longer than 10 football fields and as tall as a 22-story building. These and other limestone chambers are the largest and most magnificent in the world. Where do you think Carlsbad Caverns is located? Take a look.

Why? A fiery explosion jolted the desert near Alamogordo on July 16, 1945. The heat in the fireball was hotter than that of the sun, and surrounding sand was turned to glass. A mushroom-shaped cloud appeared over the site, and that one experimental explosion changed the course of the world's history forever. Why was this event so very important?
(answer: The explosion was the first atom bomb and the beginning of the nuclear age.)

Make a movie in your mind. Picture a large hat in the middle of the floor. What kind of hat is it? It's a *sombrero* and someone's dancing around the hat. Who's doing the dancing? Why, it's *Santa Claus*. When you think of New Mexico, think of a sombrero. Sombrero = New Mexico, and Santa Claus = Santa Fe. Santa Fe, New Mexico.

NAVAJO FRY BREAD

The Navajo culture is an important part of the rich New Mexico traditions. Everyone will want a second helping of these yummy rounds of bread.

Here's what you need:

4 cups flour
1 cup powdered milk
8 teaspoons baking powder
2 teaspoons salt
2 cups warm water
cooking oil

Here's what you do:

Mix dry ingredients well and then add the water gradually. Use your hands (clean ones, of course!) to knead into a soft dough, but not sticky. Pinch off pieces of the dough and pat out into 2-inch circles about 1/4 inch thick. Ask an adult to help you fry them in hot oil until brown, turning once. Drain on a paper towel and take your choice — sprinkle lightly with salt, or spread with your favorite jam or honey. Delicious!

C A T C H A C L U E

There are over 130 towns in New Mexico that are but shadows of themselves. These and some other towns of the Old West are called
(a) retirement centers
(b) sanctuaries
(c) ghost towns.
(answer: (c); clue: shadows = ghost towns)

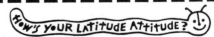

How's your Latitude Attitude?

Are Santa Fe, New Mexico and Tokyo, Japan on the same approximate latitude (35°N) as Oklahoma City, Oklahoma or Dallas, Texas?

Do you know where the biggest hole in the ground in the world is located? It's in Bingham, Utah, and it's the largest open pit copper mine in North America. Do you have a copper or penny-colored crayon? If you color Utah on your America map the color of copper, it will help you to remember what metal is mined in Bingham Canyon. It's copper!

It's no surprise that hundreds of motion pictures and T.V. shows have been shot on location in Utah. It's the perfect Old West setting with its plateaus and plains, mountains and painted deserts, and canyons. Native Americans, Mormon pioneers, and covered wagon trains heading west gave the *Beehive State* its rich heritage. Today, the Utah Jazz of the NBA and the state's tourism upsurge are giving Utah's "people of the mountains," as called by the Ute Indians, something to cheer about.

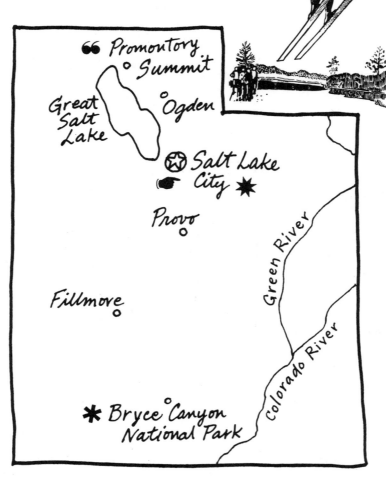

A canyon is a valley cut by moving water. There are a lot of canyons in Utah. Have you heard of the Grand Canyon in Arizona? Do you know of any other canyons in the United States, maybe one close to your home?

PACK YOUR BAGS Have you ever been stuck in waist-deep powder snow? Grab a handful, and you'll feel that the powder has such low moisture you hardly even get wet. If you're in too far, you'll need help getting out! That's what makes Utah's skiing so great. It's the powder! Names like Sundance, Snowbird, Alta, Brighton, and Park City are known to skiers around the world for the powder that makes them famous and fun to ski.

PICTURE THIS

Picture a square chunk taken out of a rectangle at the northeast corner. It looks like a one gallon fuel can without a handle, and it could be receiving some gasoline from Idaho. The spout is on the northwest corner.

THE CURIOUS W's

Who? As soon as I looked over the valley from where I stood, I knew that this would be the place to settle and build a city. I had led the pioneers through unbelievable hardships from Nauvoo, Illinois to Salt Lake Valley. I was the Mormon religious leader and territorial governor who laid out the plans for Salt Lake City. Who am I?
(answer: Brigham Young)

What? The acoustics are so finely tuned in this domed oval structure that if you listen carefully you can hear a pin drop from nearly anywhere inside. Built entirely of white pine and no nails, this unique building houses the Mormon Tabernacle Choir whose Sunday morning radio broadcast is the longest playing program on American radio. What is this structure?
(answer: the Tabernacle; Salt Lake City)

Where? "Red rocks standing like men in a bowl-shaped canyon," is how the Paiute Indians described Utah's first national park. Peek-a-boo Canyon, Silent City, Fairyland, and Wall Street are some of the marvelous formations in shades of red, pink, and cream. Where is Bryce Canyon National Park?
(answer: southwest Utah)

Why? "The last rail is laid. The last spike is driven. The Pacific railroad is finished," was the message the telegraph operator tapped out in May, 1869. The last spike was a golden one, and Promontory Summit was instantly a place of great national importance. Do you know why?
(answer: The Union Pacific and Central Pacific railroads met here, completing the first transcontinental railroad in the United States.)

Make a movie in your mind. Picture a crazy driver in the middle of the road. He's making a *U-turn*. And what's that on top of his car? It's a little *kitty*. Look out! He just drove into the *Great Salt Lake*. Ohhh! that salt tastes terrible. Now you know the capital of the state of Utah. U-turn = Utah and Great Salt Lake + kitty = Salt Lake City.

In days of old, families had a crest or coat of arms. It would be in the shape of a shield, with three or four sections depicting things the family was well known for such as sports, business or trade, special family achievements, where they lived.

Make a crest for your home state or for a state you would like to visit. For Utah, your crest might show the Great Salt Lake, a seagull for the state bird, a beehive for the state nickname, a lily for the state flower, a beautiful canyon - or whatever about Utah strikes your fancy. You can draw your crest on some construction paper, or better yet, cut a shield out of some cardboard, and paint your crest with tempera paints.

MAKE A STATE CREST

DID YOU KNOW ?

The Great Salt Lake is 4-5 times saltier than the oceans. That's because the lake is not drained by any out-flowing streams. Water drains into the lake, and then evaporates, leaving the heavier salt to sink to the bottom, because it has no place to go. The only saltier body of water in the world is the Dead Sea.

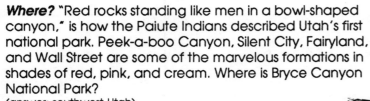
Ⓒ Ⓐ Ⓣ Ⓒ Ⓗ Ⓐ Ⓒ Ⓛ Ⓤ Ⓔ

Between 1856 and 1861, about 4,000 people walked almost hand-in-hand along the Mormon Trail. Their main means of carrying their belongings were
(a) horses
(b) covered wagons
(c) handcarts.
(answer: (c); clue; hand = handcarts)

COLOR AMERICA!

French trappers called regions of the Grand Canyon, "Pierre Jaune," which translates to yellow stone, because the walls of the deep canyon are different shades of yellow-colored stone. Could you find a yellow for Wyoming on your America! map that might be the color of the canyon walls?

Ⓞur nation's oldest national park with its erupting geysers and thousands of hot springs make Wyoming one of the world's most magnificent tourist attractions. In addition to Yellowstone, Wyoming's scenic splendor is also found in its vast prairies and towering mountains. Names of Flaming Gorge, the Red Desert, East of Eden, Devils Tower, and Firehole Canyon describe incredible natural wonders. With its treasure of dinosaur bones and fossils, Wyoming's ancient past helps us to see our land as it used to be.

MAPTALK

A gorge is a narrow canyon with steep walls. Can you locate a gorge on the map? Try looking in Wyoming for Flaming Gorge or Colorado for the Royal Gorge. Most gorges are natural, but sometimes they are manmade. One thing is for sure – they are all gorge-ous!

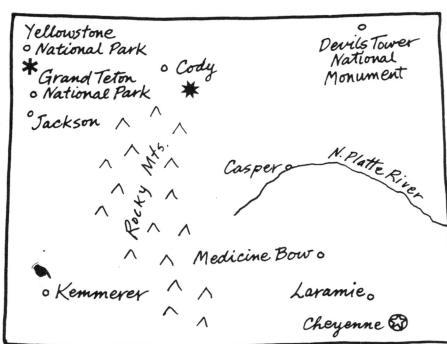

Yellowstone
o National Park

o Devils Tower National Monument

✳ Grand Teton
o National Park   o Cody

o Jackson

Rocky Mts.

Casper o   N. Platte River

Medicine Bow o

o Kemmerer   Laramie o

Cheyenne

PICTURE THIS

Wyoming is almost a square, bowed in a little from the north by the weight of Montana to the north.

THE CURIOUS W's

 Who? I hold the record for the longest Pony Express ride ever. When I was 15 years old, I rode 322 miles in Wyoming because my replacement had been killed! I founded the city of Cody, and I got my nickname by shooting 4,862 buffalo in one season. Who am I?
(answer: William "Buffalo Bill" Cody; born in Iowa but spent many years in Cody)

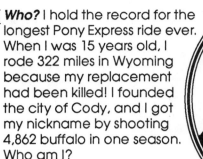

👉 **What?** He went west and became a partner in a dry goods store in Kemmerer. The store prospered, and within six years, he owned a chain of five stores. Today, his department store is a household name. What is its name?
(answer: J.C. Penney Co., founded by James Cash Penney; Kemmerer)

✳ **Where?** Devastating fires swept through Yellowstone National Park in 1988, but naturalists now believe that it may emerge better than ever. Can you find this home of the geyser, Old Faithful?
(answer: north of Jackson and Grand Teton National Park)

 Why? The Great Divide Basin is an unusual feature of the Continental Divide. Why is the Great Divide Basin so unique?
(answer: Its waters don't flow in either direction — east or west. They simply don't go anywhere.)

 Make a movie in your mind. Look up into the sky, and picture a flock of *homing* pigeons. *Why* are they flying home? They're flying home to see Ann, who is so shy that they call her *shy Ann*. You now know the capital of Wyoming. Shy Ann = Cheyenne and why + homing = Wyoming. Cheyenne, Wyoming!

STATE STUMPERS

The only thing needed to play this fast-moving game is a good imagination. One person begins by naming a state. The rest of the players go in turn and name anything that begins with the same letter as the first letter of the state. Allow no more than five seconds to come up with an answer. If you get stumped, you are out! Last one still playing is the winner and gets to pick the next state. You can decide ahead if any object can be named, or if the game is to be limited to special categories such as animals (including birds and fish), or only manmade objects, or food, etc. Think up your own variations. Let's see now. If we were naming any animal and someone said, "Arkansas," what would you say. . . an armadillo?

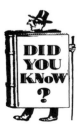 Two Ocean Pass got its name for a most unusual reason. When the water level is high, the water from two creeks comes together. One creek rushes toward the Pacific Ocean and the other creek sends its water to the Atlantic Ocean. Amazing, isn't it? Can you guess why this happens? Clue: The Continental Divide.

PACK YOUR BAGS

It's Frontier Days, and it's as wild and wooly as any Old West celebration could ever be. Wyomingites and out-of-staters come to Cheyenne in July for the nine-day celebration that hosts one of the all-time great American rodeos. Indian dancing and ceremonies, parades, demonstrations, music, and other entertainment, are reminders of Wyoming's cowboy and Native American past. What a grand celebration it is!

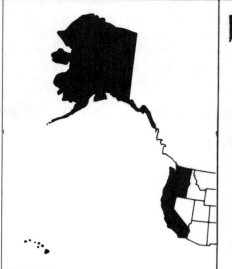

THE PACIFIC STATES

NAME THE CAPITAL

How many capitals of the Pacific states can you name? Write the names below, then check your answers on the state maps. Each state capital is marked with a ✪. Did you get all five state capitals correct?

ALASKA _____

CALIFORNIA _____

HAWAII _____

OREGON _____

WASHINGTON _____

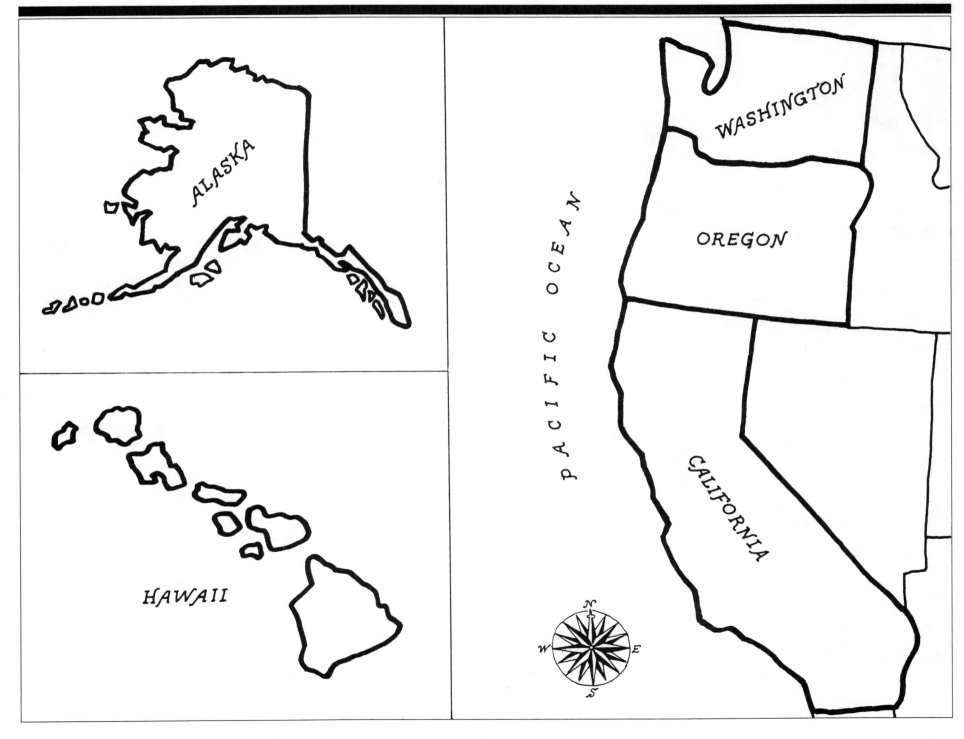

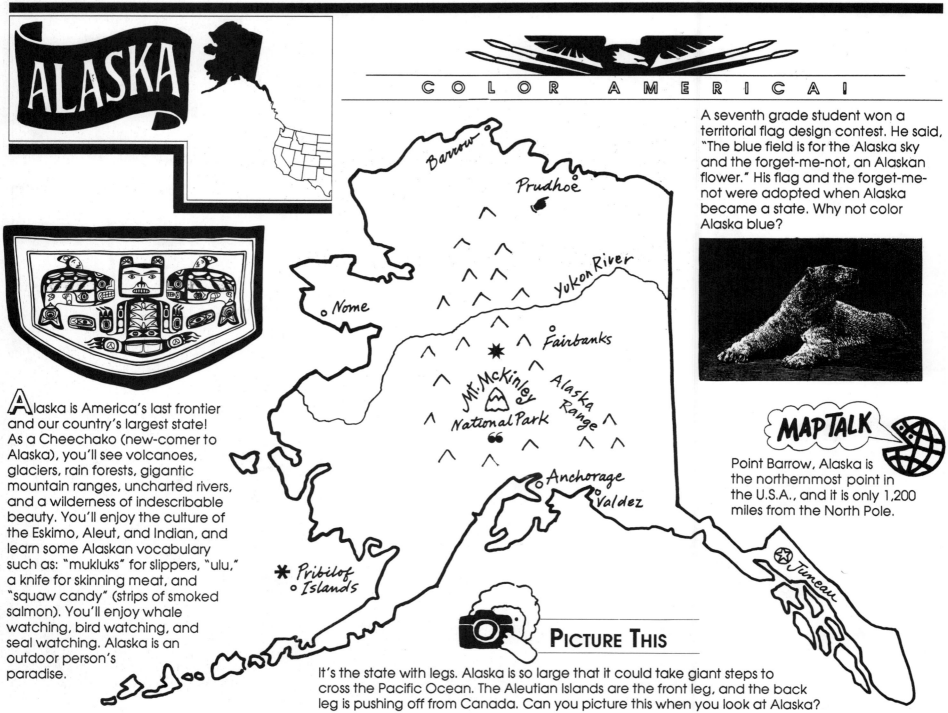

ALASKA

COLOR AMERICA!

A seventh grade student won a territorial flag design contest. He said, "The blue field is for the Alaska sky and the forget-me-not, an Alaskan flower." His flag and the forget-me-not were adopted when Alaska became a state. Why not color Alaska blue?

Alaska is America's last frontier and our country's largest state! As a Cheechako (new-comer to Alaska), you'll see volcanoes, glaciers, rain forests, gigantic mountain ranges, uncharted rivers, and a wilderness of indescribable beauty. You'll enjoy the culture of the Eskimo, Aleut, and Indian, and learn some Alaskan vocabulary such as: "mukluks" for slippers, "ulu," a knife for skinning meat, and "squaw candy" (strips of smoked salmon). You'll enjoy whale watching, bird watching, and seal watching. Alaska is an outdoor person's paradise.

MAP TALK

Point Barrow, Alaska is the northernmost point in the U.S.A., and it is only 1,200 miles from the North Pole.

PICTURE THIS

It's the state with legs. Alaska is so large that it could take giant steps to cross the Pacific Ocean. The Aleutian Islands are the front leg, and the back leg is pushing off from Canada. Can you picture this when you look at Alaska?

Map labels: Barrow, Prudhoe, Nome, Yukon River, Fairbanks, Mt. McKinley, Alaska Range, National Park, Anchorage, Valdez, Pribilof Islands, Juneau

THE CURIOUS W's

★ **Who?** I purchased Alaska for two cents an acre for the United States, and that was a great bargain even in 1867. Of course, many people thought I was crazy, and they called Alaska "Seward's Folly" and "Seward's Icebox." I'm considered to be one of the state's founding fathers, but I've never set foot on the land! Who am I?
(answer: William Seward)

☞ **What?** I extend from Prudho to Valdez for 800 miles, and I'm not a river or a highway. Sometimes I'm below the ground, and other times I'm above. I transport "black gold" to tankers and refineries, and what I transport just might end up in your car! What's the name of this vast structure?
(answer: the Alaska Pipeline)

✳ **Where?** Talk about crowded conditions! A million and a half Pacific fur seals breed on the Pribilof Islands every year. That's not all. The islands are also home to over 100 million birds of over 180 species! Bring your binoculars to see this amazing sight. Can you find the Pribilof Islands?
(answer: 200 miles north of the Aleutian Islands)

❝ **Why?** Mount Everest may be taller by about 8,700 feet, but Mount McKinley is one of America's magnificent showpieces. Why is Mount McKinley an important feature of America's geography?
(answer: It's the tallest peak in the U.S. and all of North America.)

ALASKA

How Big?

And just how big is Alaska? Big. Colossal. Gigantic. Enormous. Did you know that it's about the same distance across Alaska as it is from San Diego, California, to Savannah, Georgia? A whopping 2,400 miles. Now, that's big. Can you find these two cities on the map and see for yourself?

LIGHTS, CAMERA, ACTION!

Make a movie in your mind. When you think of Alaska picture an *igloo* made with blocks of ice. Igloo = Alaska. Now picture an Eskimo tacking a large June calendar on the front of his igloo, and he's circling the word *"June"* with a bold, black "O," because it's almost summertime. June + O = Juneau the capital. Juneau, Alaska!

EARTH TALK

You don't need 20/20 vision to see the highest spot in the United States, but what if you had to measure Mt. McKinley with a yardstick, 3 feet at a time? It would take years! Thank goodness someone has already done the measuring, and you can remember how high it is by thinking of your 20/20 vision and that yardstick. Picture the yardstick (3') as the slash in 20/20, that is 20-3-20. Now you can remember the highest point in the whole U.S.A. It's 20,320 feet high. Start climbing!

L•E•G•E•N•D & L•I•G•H•T•S

Eskimo legend says that the streams of light across the Alaskan winter night sky are the spirits of the dead playing ball with a walrus head! Scientists have several explanations, but no one really knows for sure what causes the brilliant, Fourth-of-July-like explosions of color. The mysterious Northern Lights are called the *aurora borealis*. Wouldn't you love to hop on a plane and see this strange spectacular light show in person?

PACK YOUR BAGS

Snow. Snow. Snow. What do you do in all that snow? Well, you can play golf on the frozen Bering Sea, or you can play snowshoe baseball. For the super adventurous, you can be flown into untouched slopes of the finest powder snow, by helicopter, for a day of swooshing down the mountains. Or, hop on an excursion boat and visit some of the 20 glaciers in Prince William Sound. Alaska is a wonderland of excitement.

Author! Author!

Some real-life situations are so exciting that it's hard to believe they are true. Well, here's an event that happens once every year in Alaska. Why not grab a paper and pencil, curl up in a comfortable spot, and let your imagination run wild. Here's the situation:

Yelping, barking, restless dogs are everywhere. Excitement is in the air, and anticipation of winning is at a peak. It's Alaska. It's March. It's the world-famous Iditarod Trail Sled Dog Race, named after a ghost town. You'll head out from Anchorage, and your destination is 1,160 miles away in Nome. You and your 19 dogs have practiced all year. You recall during one practice session being attacked by a starving moose, so you keep a rifle handy in case it happens again. You've been chosen number one, and you're first out of the chute. The sled glides along the freshly fallen snow. Six hours later you feel the temperature drop. The slight wind is changing into a gale, and your dogs are beginning to stiffen. A coating of ice has formed on their muzzles and your own limbs become numb. It is snowing so hard that you can't see the lead dog. You know that the trip will take 11 to 18 days, and you want to win the $50,000 first prize. Just imagine the rest of this trip. How can you stay on course in the blinding, freezing snow? How can you keep your dogs and yourself alive, much less win the race?

The Big Spill

When a tanker carrying 1.2 million barrels of crude oil went aground, the whole world took notice. The Exxon Valdez, heading for California,was 25 miles out from the Alaska coast in Prince William Sound when disaster struck. In the wee morning hours of March 24, 1989, the tanker hit a reef, ripping and tearing huge gashes in the hull, and then the oil began to spill. It gushed out at 20,000 gallons an hour, and when it was finished, the oil slick was over 8 miles long and 4 miles wide. It was the worst environmental disaster in U.S. history.

Seals, otters, whales, dolphins, and porpoises were covered with the thick goop. Birds couldn't fly because their wings were coated and heavy; fish couldn't swim. Ducks and sea lions were washed ashore, covered with the crude oil. The ecology of Prince William Sound had been changed, maybe forever. Millions of wildlife creatures died, and the world wonders if that once beautiful refuge will ever be the same. What could you suggest so that this kind of disaster won't happen again?

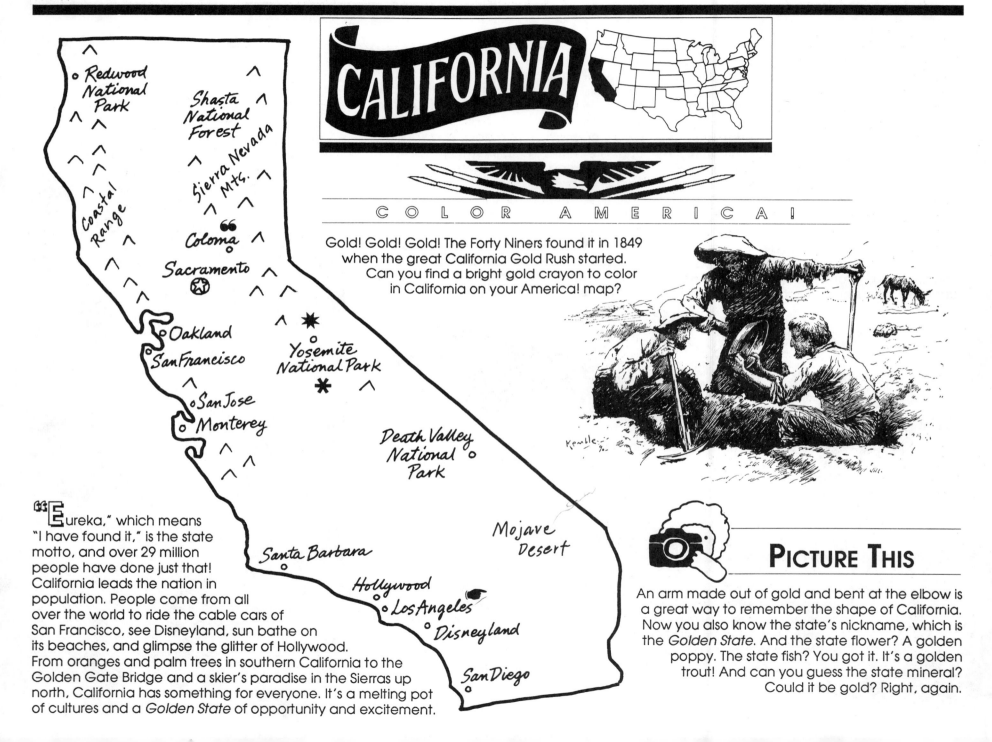

CALIFORNIA

COLOR AMERICA!

Gold! Gold! Gold! The Forty Niners found it in 1849 when the great California Gold Rush started. Can you find a bright gold crayon to color in California on your America! map?

Map Labels
- Redwood National Park
- Shasta National Forest
- Sierra Nevada Mts.
- Coastal Range
- Coloma
- Sacramento ☆
- Oakland
- San Francisco
- San Jose
- Monterey
- Yosemite National Park
- Death Valley National Park
- Mojave Desert
- Santa Barbara
- Hollywood
- Los Angeles
- Disneyland
- San Diego

"Eureka," which means "I have found it," is the state motto, and over 29 million people have done just that! California leads the nation in population. People come from all over the world to ride the cable cars of San Francisco, see Disneyland, sun bathe on its beaches, and glimpse the glitter of Hollywood. From oranges and palm trees in southern California to the Golden Gate Bridge and a skier's paradise in the Sierras up north, California has something for everyone. It's a melting pot of cultures and a *Golden State* of opportunity and excitement.

PICTURE THIS

An arm made out of gold and bent at the elbow is a great way to remember the shape of California. Now you also know the state's nickname, which is the *Golden State*. And the state flower? A golden poppy. The state fish? You got it. It's a golden trout! And can you guess the state mineral? Could it be gold? Right, again.

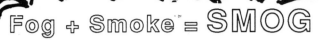

Fog + Smoke = SMOG

Because of so many automobiles in Los Angeles, plus the factories, the trucks, and all kinds of industry, something forms when fog and smoke mix. It's called smog, and it's not only California's problem, but a growing concern throughout the world. California is doing many things about smog. Most automobiles in the state must have an emissions control device that limits the amount of exhaust fumes emitted into the air. Do you have smog in the area where you live? Is something being done to clean up the air?

WHOSE FAULT IS IT?

A 5 on this scale can be destructive. A 2 on this scale can hardly be felt. A 7 or 8 can be devastating. You've heard of it. It's called the *Richter Scale*, and it measures the power of an earthquake. A 5 on the Richter scale is 10 times more powerful than a 4. It's 100 times more powerful at 6 than at 4. Can you figure out how many times greater the power of an earthquake is at 7 than at 4? You're right if you said 1,000 times more powerful. Check the newspaper next time you hear of an earthquake and see how powerful it was. There's a large, destructive earthquake somewhere in the world about every 2 weeks, but most happen under the ocean and are unnoticed. Remember where earthquakes happen? On faults!

 In Northern California, if you hop on a San Francisco cable car, the first thing you do is hold on! You'll loose your breath going up and down those steep hills heading toward Fisherman's Wharf. Once you're there you will see pots of steaming crabs and stacked loaves of sourdough French bread at the open-air fish markets. There's a boat trip around the bay which takes you past the old prison, Alcatraz, and the Golden Gate Bridge and Treasure Island. Chinatown is the largest of its kind in the world, outside of the Orient, and everyone is invited to the exciting Chinese New Year celebration.

What's there to do in Southern California? Well, for starters, Disneyland seems to be the main attraction with wonderful places like Knott's Berry Farm, Universal Studios, and 21 miles out in the Pacific is Catalina Island. Surf and sand describe the L.A.

beaches, and movie stars and Hollywood have been a team since the first silent movies. The closer to Mexico, the more south-of-the-border customs and culture you'll see, all reflecting California's Spanish and Mexican ties. You'll hear Spanish being spoken, and the Mexican food is "muy delicioso." Very delicious.

Make a movie in your mind. In California you'd better eat your vegetables if you want to remember the state capital, Sacramento. Sacramento = *sack of tomatoes* and California = *cauliflower*. Picture opening up a grocery sack of red, juicy tomatoes and an enormous cauliflower. Sack of tomatoes + cauliflower = Sacramento, California!

THE CURIOUS W's

Who? I once rode a glacier 2,500 feet down to the canyon floor of Yosemite National Park! I'm an explorer, naturalist, and writer. I have been described as the Father of Yosemite, and I spent my lifetime enticing others into the wilderness. Who am I?
(answer: John Muir; the national monument is Muir Woods)

What? Skeletal remains of a saber-toothed cat, prehistoric bear, ground sloths, wolves, llamas, mammoths, and mastodons were found here beneath oozing, bubbling, black tar. They were trapped millions of years ago, when they came to pools to drink. What is this prehistoric burial ground?
(answer: La Brea Tar Pits; Hancock Park, Los Angeles)

Where? Spectacular waterfalls and gigantic granite cliffs with names of El Capitan and Half Dome are some of the most photographed natural wonders of our country. Its deep canyons and snow-capped peaks, rivers, waterfalls, and valleys make this national park a California and an American treasure. Look east of San Francisco to locate Yosemite National Park.

Why? What I carried in my handkerchief that rainy morning changed the history of California. There were just a few small nuggets of a bright gold mineral, but John Sutter, the owner of the sawmill where I worked, and I both knew what I'd discovered. It was gold! Why did this discovery change California?
(answer: The California Gold Rush of 1849 started a migration of people that has never stopped; Coloma)

★ — NATURE'S SUPER STARS — ★

Mount Whitney is the tallest mountain in the contiguous United States and *Death Valley* is the lowest point in the continental United States. The *General Sherman Tree* in Sequoia National Park is the largest tree in the world (a whopping 102' around its base), but it's not the tallest. The *Howard Libbey Redwood* in Humboldt County is the tallest tree in the world, topping out at 362'. But wait, that's not all . . . The *bristlecone pines* are the oldest trees in the world, dating back over 4,000 years.

JUST IMAGINE

The hot dog that I was about to sink my teeth into smelled delicious. It was Game Three of the World Series, and I was sitting with my dad about 150 feet up from the playing field at Candlestick Park in San Francisco. The Giants and the Oakland A's were warming up for the game, and suddenly, at 5:04 P.M., the concrete beneath my feet began to move for several seconds, while the stadium swayed and shook. There was a rumbling noise, like a jet plane taking off. It was an earthquake! I had never been in an earthquake before, and it was scary. On my dad's pocket radio, we heard that a section of the Bay Bridge had fallen into the ocean and that a level of a freeway had collapsed. Brick buildings fell down and fires started. The whole city was in chaos. Just imagine . . . my first World Series and my first earthquake, all on the same night. It was October 17, 1989. Can you put yourself in my seat and just imagine what it would have been like?

• JOIN • THE • WATER • SAVERS •

California has experienced a serious drought in the 1980s and 90s, but everybody should be trying to conserve this precious natural resource. Here's a simple way for each person to save a whopping 126 gallons of water per week. *Turn off the water while you are actually brushing your*

teeth. Turn the water on only to wet your toothbrush and to quickly rinse your mouth and toothbrush when finished. Here's a silly little jingle that you can "think" while rinsing: "Up like a rocket, down like the rain, back and forth like a choo-choo train." When you finish "thinking" the jingle, the water should be off. Give it a try and help save America's water!

TAKE ME OUT TO THE BALL GAME . . .

But first you just have to figure out which one. California leads the nation in professional sports teams. The Los Angeles Dodgers, San Francisco Giants, San Diego Padres, Oakland Athletics, and the California Angels all call California home. Think of the hot dogs that are sold when California's five major league baseball teams play in their home stadiums!

When it comes to basketball there is Earvin "Magic" Johnson and the Los Angeles Lakers, the Los Angeles Clippers, the Golden State Warriors and the Sacramento Kings.

If it's football season, look for the Los Angeles Raiders, the Los Angeles Rams, the Chargers who make San Diego their home, and the San Francisco Forty Niners. Joe Montana thrills the crowds during football season, and the fans affectionately refer to him as "The golden great from the Golden Gate."

Los Angeles has hockey too, with Wayne Gretzsky and the Los Angeles Kings of the NHL. Have you decided which ball game to see?

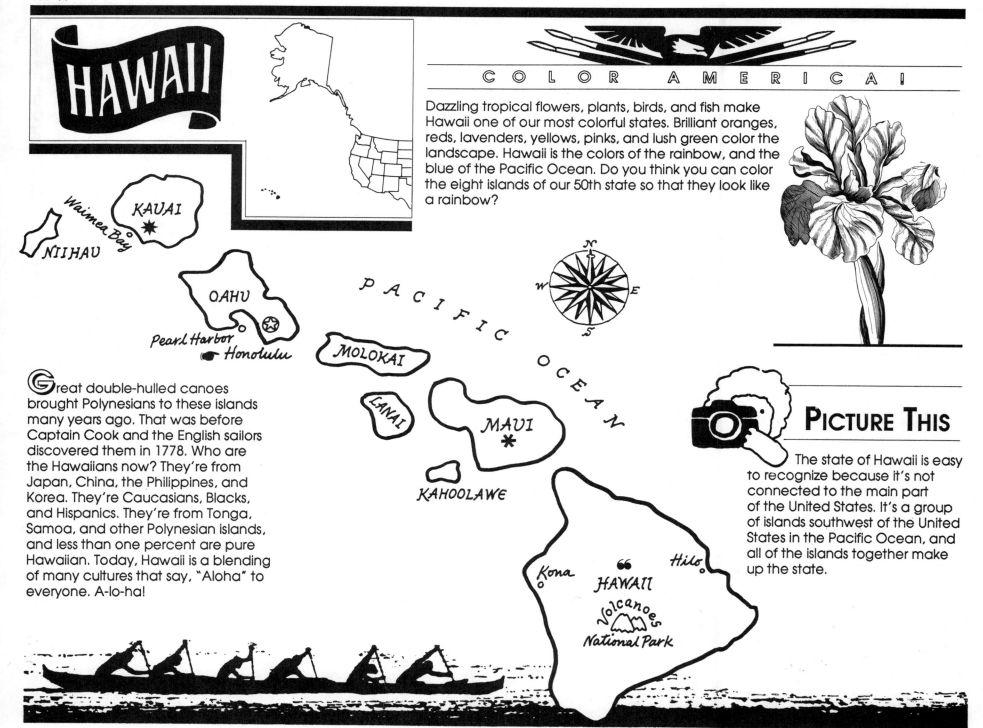

HAWAII

COLOR AMERICA!

Dazzling tropical flowers, plants, birds, and fish make Hawaii one of our most colorful states. Brilliant oranges, reds, lavenders, yellows, pinks, and lush green color the landscape. Hawaii is the colors of the rainbow, and the blue of the Pacific Ocean. Do you think you can color the eight islands of our 50th state so that they look like a rainbow?

NIIHAU

Waimea Bay

KAUAI

OAHU

Pearl Harbor

Honolulu

MOLOKAI

LANAI

MAUI

KAHOOLAWE

PACIFIC OCEAN

KONA

HAWAII

Volcanoes National Park

Hilo

Great double-hulled canoes brought Polynesians to these islands many years ago. That was before Captain Cook and the English sailors discovered them in 1778. Who are the Hawaiians now? They're from Japan, China, the Philippines, and Korea. They're Caucasians, Blacks, and Hispanics. They're from Tonga, Samoa, and other Polynesian islands, and less than one percent are pure Hawaiian. Today, Hawaii is a blending of many cultures that say, "Aloha" to everyone. A-lo-ha!

PICTURE THIS

The state of Hawaii is easy to recognize because it's not connected to the main part of the United States. It's a group of islands southwest of the United States in the Pacific Ocean, and all of the islands together make up the state.

CATCH A CLUE

What a surprise it is to know that there are 132 islands in the state of Hawaii. The largest of the eight main islands is:

(a) Kauai
(b) Oahu
(c) Hawaii.

(answer: (c); clue: Hawaii = Hawaii)

Aloha, Friends & Neighbors

Any reason is a good reason to have a luau, or Hawaiian feast. *Here's what you do:* Since it would be difficult to roast a kalua pig in a pit in your backyard, fix the food inside and carry it out! Pick a warm, summer day when fresh fruit is plentiful and make your own Hawaiian menu. A plate of sliced bananas and pineapple (canned chunks are fine), or some other fruit, along with a bowlful of steaming rice are a good start. Barbecued beef, fish, or chicken would be great, and if you brush the meat with a little teriyaki sauce, it will really have that Hawaiian flavor. Cupcakes with coconut sprinkled on top could be the final touch. Play some Hawaiian music, get everyone on their feet to dance a hula, and string leis of leaves or flowers for a headband or necklace. Great fun Hawaiian-style!

WEATHER OR NOT

"Rain, rain, go away . . ." but it hardly ever does on Mount Waialeale, because it's the rainiest spot in the entire world. The mountain is on the island of Kauai, and about 500 inches of rain fall here each year. Check the average rainfall for your city and state in the weather section of your newspaper. Where do you suppose that 500 inches of rain could go? It rains so often and so much that the water rushes down the mountainside and flows right into the Pacific Ocean!

HAWAII

LIGHTS, CAMERA, ACTION!

Make a movie in your mind. Honolulu, Hawaii is fun to say and fun to remember. What do you think of when you think of Hawaii? How about a *Hawaiian pineapple*? Yum. Picture a person-sized Hawaiian pineapple, named *Lulu*, wearing a grass skirt, dancing the *hula* with a big smile on its face. Hula + Lulu = Honolulu. Pineapple = Hawaii. Honolulu, Hawaii.

THE CURIOUS W's

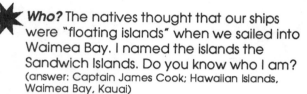

Who? The natives thought that our ships were "floating islands" when we sailed into Waimea Bay. I named the islands the Sandwich Islands. Do you know who I am?
(answer: Captain James Cook; Hawaiian Islands, Waimea Bay, Kauai)

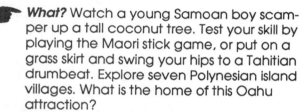

What? Watch a young Samoan boy scamper up a tall coconut tree. Test your skill by playing the Maori stick game, or put on a grass skirt and swing your hips to a Tahitian drumbeat. Explore seven Polynesian island villages. What is the home of this Oahu attraction?
(answer: The Polynesian Cultural Center; Oahu)

Where? The volcano's name is Haleakala, and it means "House of the Sun." It's a perfect name because at sunrise, the entire 3,000 foot deep crater and its rust-colored cinder cones light up with the early morning rays. This massive, dormant volcano is over 10,000' high and about 22 miles around. Can you find Haleakala National Park?
(answer: Maui)

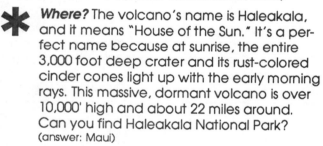

Why? Men doing the hula? That's right. The very first people to dance the hula were men. The Hawaiians did not have a written language for many years, so the hula was very important to them. Can you guess why?
(answer: It was a way to tell about their history. Watching the motions was like reading a book!)

SOMETHING'S FISHY!

Over 680 different species of tropical fish swim in the reefs around the islands, and an amazing one-third of them are native to Hawaii. This is the only place in the world where they are found.

PASS THE PEAS, PLEASE

Grab your snorkel, mask, fins, and frozen peas and head for the surf! Did someone say, "frozen peas"? Sounds strange, but the tropical fish love frozen peas. Be careful not to let too many out of your hand at once, or you'll end up in a school of friendly little black and yellow striped *kihikihis* or the little yellow *lau'i-palas*. They'll take food right out of your hand. *Mahimahis* don't come in where people snorkel, but if you meet one underwater, just smile back. A mahimahi is a dolphin!

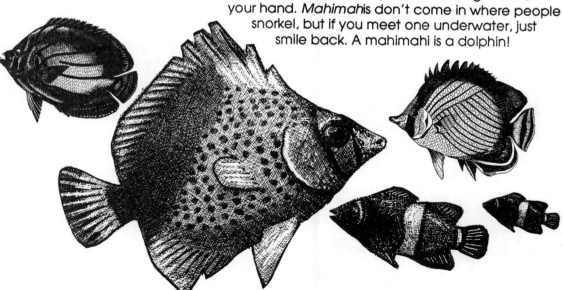

VOLCANO TRIVIA

Many of the earth's active volcanoes are found in the Ring of Fire, a zone made up of the land areas surrounding the Pacific Ocean. This is definitely a big "hot" spot that includes Mt. Lassen in California, Mt. Fuji in Japan, and many more volcanoes.

What do Mt. Pinatubo in the Philippines, Mt. Unzun in Japan, and Mt. St. Helens in Washington state, have in common? That's right, they all blew their tops in the 1980s and 1990s. They're volcanoes. Did you read about them in the newspaper?

The Hawaiian Islands are moving 10 centimeters to the northwest each year. The Hawaiian Islands were formed by hot spots underneath the earth that surfaced and created volcanic islands. Kauai was formed first, then Oahu, then Molokai, then Maui, and last of all the big island of Hawaii. What would you call the next island that might be formed one million years from today?

Leis of the Land

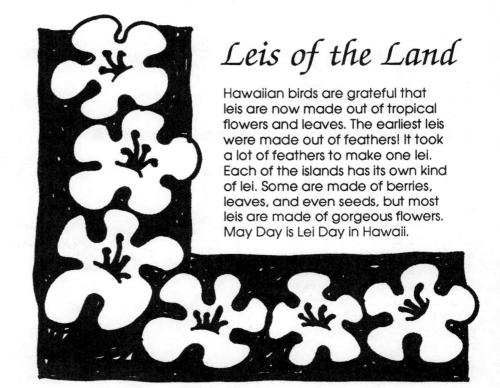

Hawaiian birds are grateful that leis are now made out of tropical flowers and leaves. The earliest leis were made out of feathers! It took a lot of feathers to make one lei. Each of the islands has its own kind of lei. Some are made of berries, leaves, and even seeds, but most leis are made of gorgeous flowers. May Day is Lei Day in Hawaii.

PACK YOUR BAGS

Every day could be a vacation day in Hawaii. The temperature in the lowlands stays between 70° and 85° all year long. Just think of what you could do. For an unusual experience, why not visit Hawaii Volcanoes National Park. The Mauna Loa and Kilauea volcanoes might even erupt while you watch! Don't worry though, because the observation areas are a safe distance away. Talk about a big welcome!

OREGON

Have you ever seen a Douglas Fir tree, the state tree of Oregon? Most of the Christmas trees sold in the western states are this kind of evergreen tree. Their symmetrical shape with lush dark green needles and fragrant smell make it the popular tree that it is. Since nearly half of Oregon is covered with dense forests, how would the whole state look colored dark green on your America! map?

Windsurfing in Hood River, salmon fishing at Astoria, crabbing near Newport, or just driving the breathtaking 400-mile coast, is Oregon at its best. The *Beaver State*, named after those pesky little tree gnawers and dam builders, brought traders to the territory for the beavers' valuable fur pelts. Pioneers packed their wagons and headed for Oregon over a route known as the Oregon Trail. These early pioneers blazed the path out of rugged wilderness from the Atlantic to the Pacific. Today, Oregonians still have that progressive, pioneer spirit.

Map labels: Columbia River, Portland, Bonneville Dam, Pendleton, Salem, Cascade Range, Hells Canyon, Eugene, Bend, Crater Lake National Park

PICTURE THIS

Whoever heard of a chicken without a beak? Take a close look at Oregon. Picture a fat hen sitting on an egg. On the Pacific Ocean side of the chicken pretend there's a beak attached at the top northwest corner, where it looks like the chicken's head. Do you see it? Cackle twice if you do.

WHAT'S A GREAT BASIN?

It's not a big bathroom sink. It's an area of land, but it still has to do with draining water, kind of like the basins in your home. Where is this Great Basin? It's located between the Rocky Mountains and the Sierra Nevada/Cascade Mountains. The water in this region uses interior drainage like your bathroom basin with all the water eventually ending up draining into the Great Salt Lake. Try to find the Great Basin on a map.

THE CURIOUS W's

Who? Can fish climb ladders? They do at this enormous structure on the Columbia River. The fish are salmon, and they're swimming up manmade ladders to go upstream to lay their eggs. The ladders, or steps, are the only way of getting them past this concrete structure. What's the name of this mass of concrete?
(answer: Bonneville Dam)

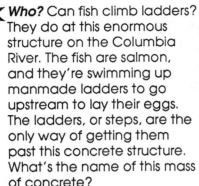

Where? Astronauts used this area as a training ground, walking on lava rocks in the volcanic, moon-like terrain. There's a 500' cinder cone and lava cast trees. The lava casts are what remain after oozing, hot lava burned a forest of pine trees, leaving the casts where live trees once stood. Where is Lava Lands?
(answer: Find Bend and you'll be close.)

Why? When a prospector was looking for the Lost Cabin Mine, he came upon a spectacular sight. The intense blue color of the water caused John Hillman and his mining friends to name their find, Deep Blue Lake. It was later named Crater Lake. Do you know why it's a first in our nation's lakes?
(answer: It's the deepest lake in the United States at 1,932 feet.)

Did you know that the ocean tastes salty? The reason is because the earth deposits minerals into the water and the evaporation of the water increases the concentration of the minerals. Do you remember the inland lake that has lots of salt in it? You're right, it's the Great Salt Lake in Utah.

Make a movie in your mind. Do you think that sailing in a boat is the best way to cross the Pacific Ocean? Right, unless you want to learn Oregon's capital. Picture sailing on a church organ, bobbing up and down on the waves, with a red letter "M" on the white *sail* above the *organ*. Look closely. Can you see who's playing the organ? Why, it's a smiling beaver! Sail + "M" = Salem. Organ = Oregon. Salem, Oregon. And the state's nickname? The Beaver State.

Make a Collage

Pick a state you would love to visit some day, or pick your home state and make a super collage. *Here's what you need:* lots of old magazines and catalogs, big piece of posterboard, scissors and glue. *Here's what you do:* Make a list of all the attractions, products, feelings, words, places that tell a lot about your state. Then cut out pictures, letters, words that all add up to what the state is all about. Paste everything - overlapping and in fanciful ways - on the posterboard, so that you can't see a speck of board. Glue on letters that spell the state's name. And there you have it - the next best thing to being there yourself!

"Ride 'em cowboy!" and "Head 'em out" are still sayings of the Old West and the Pendleton Round-Up carries on the tradition. Lots of folks think it's the best four days of the year when rodeo riders from all over the country head to northeastern Oregon for one of the biggest western rodeos in the world. Tepee villages are set up on the Umatilla River by Pacific Northwest Indian tribes. Pack trains, stagecoaches, handcarts, and ox teams pull into town carrying prospectors, pioneers, miners, cowboys. What an exciting weekend right out of the Old West . . . pardner.

WASHINGTON

Delicious, Winesaps, Rome Beauty, Jonathan, Golden Delicious, and McIntosh all have something in common. They're apples! Washington's got tons and tons of apples. Yellow, green, red, sweet, and tart - they're all apples. What's your favorite apple? How about coloring Washington on your America! map your favorite apple color. Did you know that Washington grows more apples than any place in the world?

With a gigantic blast, Mount St. Helens roared into life changing the look of the Cascade mountain range, just the way other volcanoes have done in the past. But there's more to Washington than volcanoes. Apples, daffodils (50 million per year), and lots of wheat, meat, potatoes, and timber fill the fertile fields. Ferryboats wind in and out of Puget Sound and the San Juan Islands, and the sandy shores keep shellers and clammers occupied. Nisqually, Stillaguamish, Skookumchuck, and many other rivers flow through lush forests, rugged terrain, and parks. Welcome to Washington, the *Evergreen State*.

PICTURE THIS

You can't miss Washington. It's the only state that has a large waterway trickling into its northwest corner. It's right at the top of the map on your left. See it? It's Puget Sound. Now take a look at all of the other states, and you'll see that there's nothing even close to the shape of Washington. Water and Washington go together.

PACK YOUR BAGS

Pack a lunch, saddle up, and you're off for a fantastic ride. There are hundreds of miles of horse trails through the mountains of Washington, especially in the three national parks, Mount Rainier, North Cascades, and Olympic.

WHO SAID THAT?

A famous campaign slogan during the election of 1844 was over a boundary dispute. "Fifty-four forty or fight" was the cry of the Democrats who wanted the Oregon Territory boundary set at 54°40' latitude. James K. Polk won the election; he compromised, and they didn't fight!

THE CURIOUS W's

👉 *What?* It's as high as a 46-story building, the largest concrete dam and the greatest single source of water power in the United States. It's three times as large as the Great Pyramid in Egypt, and it has enough concrete to build a 2-lane highway from New York to Seattle. What am I?
(answer: Grand Coulee Dam)

✳ *Where?* Mountain climbers take this mountain seriously. Its summit is over 14,000', and danger is always present. The lower elevations are great for family hiking, wildlife watching, and guided nature walks. Where is Mount Rainier?
(answer: southeast of Olympia)

❝ *Why?* You'll know my name. I'm George Bush, but I'm not the President, and my middle name is Washington. Blacks weren't allowed to settle below the Columbia River, so I did something else! Why am I important to Washington's history?
(answer: I started the first American settlement in Washington, at Tumwater.)

LIGHTS, CAMERA, ACTION!

Make a movie in your mind. Washington is the only state with the name of a U.S. President, so. . . think of George *Washington*. Now picture George in the *Olympic* games as a high jumper, clearing the bar as people in the stadium are cheering wildly. Olympics = Olympia. George Washington = Washington. Olympia, Washington.

Start Your Own Fruit Factory

Washington is known as a leading producer of many fruits and berries, and here's a good use for most kinds. Fruit leather is a cinch to make and you can be sure it will be eaten quickly!

Here's what you need: Fully ripe, firm fruit, such as peaches, apricots, plums, berries (wash and core, if necessary, but don't peel); honey; cookie sheets, plastic wrap, fine-meshed screen or lightweight cloth, such as cheesecloth.

Here's what you do: Measure the fruit, and for each cup of fruit add 1 tablespoon of honey. Puree in a blender or mix with a heavy duty type mixer or food mill until smooth. Line a cookie sheet with plastic wrap and spread the thick mixture about 1/8" - 1/4" thick on the plastic. Place the pan in direct sunlight and, if necessary, cover with screen or lightweight cheesecloth to keep the bugs away, being careful not to touch the fruit. Drying time is about 6 -12 hours depending on the heat of the sun and the humidity. It's ready to roll up or eat when it is no longer sticky on top. It may take more than one day to completely dry a batch, but less than five minutes to eat, once everyone finds out how good it is. Are you ready to take orders?

SURPRISE!

The tallest totem pole in the world is 105' high, and it is found in Tacoma, Washington . . . not in Alaska!

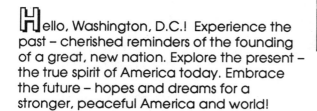

TAKE A "WALKING TOUR" OF WASHINGTON

Hello, Washington, D.C.! Experience the past – cherished reminders of the founding of a great, new nation. Explore the present – the true spirit of America today. Embrace the future – hopes and dreams for a stronger, peaceful America and world!

Take a tour of our nation's capital by "visiting" some of America's favorite landmarks. Look for the clues and see how well you'll do at matching them with a famous landmark.

★ How would you like to make $22.5 million a day, have a one hundred thousand dollar bill, and have money printed in sheets? And, guess what? Dollar bills are not made of paper; they're made of cloth – 75% cotton and 25% linen. Can you find where all of this does happen every day? (Bureau of Engraving and Printing)

★ There's a secret cave under me. I'm 19' high and weigh 150 tons, and it's all solid. Around me there are 36 columns representing the states in the Union at the time of my death. Martin Luther King gave his "I Have a Dream" speech on my steps in 1963. What do you think I am? (Lincoln Memorial)

★ I am 2,000 feet long, and at one end, I can see Lincoln, and at the other end, I can see the Washington Monument. Can you discover what I am? (The Reflecting Pool)

★ I have 897 steps leading up to the top of me, but everyone has to ride up on an elevator that gets there in just 70 seconds. I sway $1/8$" when the wind blows 35 miles per hour, and I'm 555 feet 5 inches tall, the tallest monument in the city. What am I? (Washington Monument)

★ There are the Blue Room, the Red Room, and the Green Room. In fact, there are 132 rooms. The famous address is 1600 Pennsylvania Avenue. Find this famous residence. (White House)

★ In front, there are 16 columns made of Vermont marble, each 3 stories high. The bronze doors weigh 26 tons, and inside there are 9 judges called Justices making important decisions about the laws of our country. Find this building. (The Supreme Court Building)

★ You can see the smallest book in the world here — just the size of an ant – plus a copy of the Gutenberg Bible, the first book ever printed in moveable type. This building is filled with 83 million items. Can you identify this building? (The Library of Congress)

★ If you love flags, you'll love to visit the Hall of Nations and the Hall of States with all their flags on display. Six theaters in this complex are part of this "living memorial" to one of our presidents. Can you locate it? (John F. Kennedy Center for the Performing Arts)

★ A home away from home, this memorial is patterned after the style of this President's own home, Monticello, and the University of Virginia which he founded. It has an enormous bronze statue of this President. Identify the location of this memorial. (Thomas Jefferson Memorial near the Tidal Basin)

★ You'll see handwriting being analyzed to detect forgery, shredded documents being pieced back together, tire tracks, and even shoe prints being examined and analyzed. You'll even get a sharpshooting demonstration. Where is this? (Federal Bureau of Investigation Building)

★ Shiny, black granite walls in the shape of a "V" make this memorial very unique. There are 58,132 names of the dead or missing soldiers from one of our country's longest wars, and people leave flowers, notes, war medals, and pictures beneath these names. What does this memorial honor? (Vietnam Veterans Memorial)

★ America's most precious documents, "The Declaration of Independence," "The Constitution," and "The Bill of Rights" are located here in a bombproof and fireproof vault 20' below the floor. They are sealed in glass and bronze cases filled with protective helium. Find this building. (National Archives)

★ This building is the second oldest in Washington, D.C. It houses the two chambers of Congress – the House of Representatives and the Senate. You can sit in the visitors' gallery and watch Congress in action. Where is all of this happening? (The Capitol)

★ Here you'll find a dinosaur egg that's about 70 million years old and a jaw of a great white shark that lived millions of years ago.Where are these (and many other) creatures? (Museum of Natural History; the Smithsonian Institution)

★ How would you like to see Dorothy's red slippers from the *Wizard of Oz* or the leather jacket worn by Fonzi in "Happy Days," or the boxing gloves of Muhammad Ali and Joe Louis, or the flag that flew over Ft. McHenry that inspired Francis Scott Key to write our national anthem? These things and much, much more are found in this fascinating building on The Mall.(The Museum of American History; Smithsonian Institution)

★ You can see the Kitty Hawk (plane of the Wright brothers), a replica of the space shuttle, Columbia, and the Spirit of St. Louis. Most everyone loves this place. Find it. (National Air and Space Museum; Smithsonian Institution)

★ One of our most important rights can be exercised here every day of the year. In fact, there are over 6,500 demonstrations held here each year. Sometimes it is just one person walking quietly with a sign, but other times, there are tens of thousands of people who gather to protest something or encourage our government to take action. Where does this happen? (The Mall)

★ ★ ★ ★ ★ ★ ★ ★ ★ ★ ★ ★ ★ ★

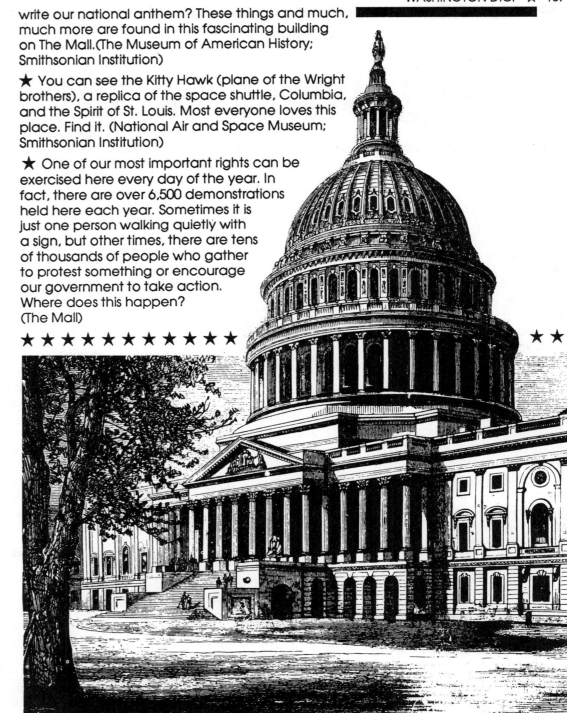

PUERTO RICO

Make a movie in your mind. Picture a beautiful *port* with sandy beaches. You're walking along the beach and you see a magician's wand made out of sand. You pick up the *sand wand*, wave it over your hat, and no rabbit comes out. So much for sand wands! Now you know the capital of Puerto Rico. Port = Puerto Rico, and sand wand = San Juan. San Juan, Puerto Rico.

¡Hola! Puerto Rico. Bordered on the north by the Atlantic Ocean and the Caribbean on the South, Puerto Rico with its rich Hispanic heritage is America's premier 100-mile-long island territory. The Puerto Ricans are self-governed, U.S. citizens.

☆ News ☆ !!!Flash!!!

Keep tuned into the news and newspapers because the U.S. Congress is considering whether to allow Puerto Rico to select to either become a state, to become independent of the U.S.(a separate country), or continue in commonwealth status. Keep posted to discover how the vote goes. How would you vote?

• IT'S IN THE NAME •

The dreaded Carib Indians were a fierce, cannibalistic people and put fear into the hearts of everyone. At one time these Indians came from South America, eventually settling in the Caribbean area. That's where the Caribbean gets its name.

PUERTO RICO'S GETTING OLDER

Island life must be very agreeable. Over a 20-year period, the average life span in Puerto Rico increased from 46 to over 70 years old. That's fantastic!

WHERE DID ALL THE SEASONS GO?

Between winter and summer in Puerto Rico, there is only about 6° difference in temperature. Can you see why it's such a favorite vacation spot?

Can you ride a *hydrocycle*? Not quite! A hydrocycle is just a fancy name that means the moving of water from the ocean, to the air, to the land, and back to the ocean. Here's the cycle:

1. Water evaporates from the world's oceans.

2. It's carried through the air and is eventually returned to the land as rain or snow.

3. The water then drains off the land into rivers and lakes and then into the sea. Isn't it amazing that water is always recycling itself?

IS IT WET OR DRY? MAYBE BOTH!

Is there any wonder that some Puerto Ricans claim that the "weather" was born here? It isn't very surprising, because the sky can send down buckets of rain, and be clear and completely dry in another 15 minutes. In Puerto Rico's El Yunque (The Anvil) rainforest, you can see a storm on one mountain and clear skies over a neighboring peak.

SUNKEN TREASURE

Treasure ships once sailed the waters of the Caribbean, their hulls filled with gold, and headed for Spain. What happened to the ones that sank? They're still there, somewhere, and treasure hunters are on the lookout.

Make a movie in your mind. Picture a girl named *Virginia* and her friend, *Charlotte*, walking along a *mall* on a small *island*. The capital of the Virgin Islands is easy when you remember: Charlotte + a mall = Charlotte Amalie and Virginia + island = Virgin Islands. Charlotte Amalie, Virgin Islands. Now that's a tongue twister!

Three sparkling jewels of the Caribbean, with the near-perfect climate, are kept breezy and warm by the trade winds. St. John, St. Thomas, and St. Croix are U.S. Territories, and the island residents are American citizens.

Who Are the Virgin Islanders?

Over three-fourths of the people are descendants of black slaves who were brought to the islands by the Europeans.

VOLCANIC FORMATION

A whole lot of shaking must have gone on when volcanoes pushed up beneath the ocean and formed the Virgin Islands. St. John, St. Thomas, and St. Croix are the three main American Virgin Islands.

WATER, WATER EVERYWHERE!

While there are oceans of water all around, there's not much on the ground in the Virgin Islands, unless it rains. There are no natural lakes or rivers, so water can be scarce. People have to conserve.

TOURIST TRADE IS TOPS

Luxurious cruise ships bring tourists who delight in the quaint shops and markets, old plantations, and lush island scenery. The white-sand beaches with their crystalline water attract people from all over the world. People agree that the view below the surf is as spectacular as the one above.

• Islands For Sale •

What a deal! The United States purchased St. John, St. Thomas, St. Croix and about 50 tiny islets in the Virgin Islands from Denmark in 1917 for $25 million. England claims the other six islands.

WEATHER OR NOT

Cyclones, hurricanes, typhoons, and tornadoes all have one thing in common and that's high winds. Are there differences among these powerful wind sources? A *cyclone* has wind that rotates in a counter-clockwise direction in the northern hemisphere, and a clockwise direction in the southern hemisphere. The earth's rotation causes this swirling motion. Hurricanes, typhoons, and tornadoes are all types of cyclones. To be called a cyclone the winds must exceed 74 miles per hour. A *hurricane* is a cyclone that is a tropical storm that builds up over warm oceans. It is accompanied by torrential rain. A hurricane is the name for the storms in the Caribbean. It's interesting that the "eye" of the hurricane is calm. It has no rain, very light winds, and clear skies. A *typhoon* is the same as a hurricane, except that it is the name given to the storms that are found in the Pacific. A *tornado* is a type of cyclone that has a funnel extending down from a large, black cloud. The updraft of air in the funnel can suck things up into it such as houses, cars, and animals. Most tornadoes occur over land, and they are often called twisters. When one happens over water, it is called a waterspout.

INDEX

To order additional copies of **Kids Learn America!**, please enclose $12.95 per copy
plus $2.50 shipping and handling. Follow "To Order" instructions on the last page. Thank you.

THE KIDS' NATURE BOOK:
365 Indoor/Outdoor Activities and Experiences
by Susan Milord

Winner of the Parents' Choice Golden Award for learning and doing books, *The Kids' Nature Book* is loved by children, grandparents, and friends alike. Simple projects and activities emphasize fun while quietly reinforcing the wonder of the world we all share.
Packed with facts and fun!

160 pages, 11 x 8½, 425 illustrations
Quality paperback, $12.95

KIDS CREATE!
Art & Craft Experiences for 3- to 9-year-olds
by Laurie Carlson

What's the most important experience for children ages 3 to 9? Why, to create something by themselves. Carlson provides over 150 creative experiences ranging from making dinosaur sculptures to clay cactus gardens, from butterfly puppets to windsocks. Plenty of help for the parents working with the kids, too! A delightfully innovative book.

160 pages, 11 x 8½, over 400 illustrations,
Quality paperback, $12.95

ADVENTURES IN ART
Art & Craft Experiences for 7- to 14-year-olds
by Susan Milord

Imagine an art book that encourages children to explore, to experience, to touch and to see, to learn and to create . . . imagine a true adventure in art. Here's a book that teaches artisans' skills without stifling creativity. Covers making handmade papers, puppets, masks, paper seascapes, seed art, tin can lantern, berry ink, still life, silk screen, batiking, carving, and so much more. Perfect for the older child. Let the adventure begin!

160 pages, 11 x 8½, 500 illustrations
Quality paperback, $12.95

KIDS AND WEEKENDS!
Exciting Ways to Make Special Days
by Avery Hart and Paul Mantell

Packed with truly creative ways to play, have fun, learn, grow, and build self-esteem and positive relationships, this book is a must for every parent, grandparent, baby-sitter, and teacher. Hart and Mantell will inspire us all to transform some part of every weekend – even if it is only 30 minutes – into a special experience. Everything from backyard nature to putting on a magic show to creating a bird sanctuary to writing a book about yourself to environmentally sound activities for indoors and out. Whatever your interests, no matter how busy you are, kids and their families will savor these special weekend moments.

176 pages, 11 x 8½, over 400 illustrations
Quality paperback, $12.95

KIDS COOK!
Fabulous Food For The Whole Family
by Sarah Williamson and Zachary Williamson

Kids Cook! is filled with over 150 recipes for great tasting foods that kids ages 8 and up can cook for themselves and for their families and friends, too. Recipes from sections like "It's the Berries!" "Pasta Perfect," "Home Alone," "Side Orders," " Baby-sitter's Bonanza," and "Best Bets for Brunch" include real foods that are fun to eat. Plus Nutri Notes, Safety First, and plenty of special menus for Father's Day, Grandma's Teatime, picnics, and parties. One terrific book!

160 pages, 11 x 8½, Over 150 recipes, illustrations
Quality paperback, $12.95

DOING CHILDREN'S MUSEUMS
A Guide to 265 Hands-On Museums
by Joanne Cleaver

Turn an ordinary day into a spontaneous "vacation" by taking a child to some of the 265 participatory children's museums, discovery rooms, and nature centers covered in this highly acclaimed, one-of-a-kind book. Filled with museum specifics to help you pick and plan the perfect place for the perfect day, Cleaver has created a most valuable resource for anyone who loves kids! New updated edition!

272 pages, 6 x 9
Quality paperback, $13.95

PARENTS ARE TEACHERS, TOO
Enriching Your Child's First Six Years
by Claudia Jones

Winner of the Parents' Choice Seal of Approval! Be the best teacher your child ever has. Jones shares hundreds of ways to help any child learn in playful home situations. Lots on developing reading, writing, math skills. Plenty on creative and critical thinking, too. A book you'll love using!

192 pages, 6 x 9, illustrations,
Quality paperback, $9.95

THE HOMEWORK SOLUTION
by Linda Agler Sonna

Put homework responsibilities where they belong - in the student's lap! Here it is! The simple remedy for the millions of parents who are tired of waging the never-ending nightly battle over kids' homework. Dr. Sonna's "One Step Solution" will relieve parents, kids, and their siblings of the ongoing problem within a single month.

192 pages, 6 x 9,
Quality paperback, $10.95

MORE PARENTS ARE TEACHERS, TOO
Encouraging Your 6- to 12-Year-Old
by Claudia Jones

Winner of the Parents' Choice Seal of Approval! Help your children be the best they can be! When parents are involved, kids do better. When kids do better, they feel better, too. Here's a wonderfully creative book of ideas, activities, teaching methods and more to help you help your children over the rough spots and share in their growing joy in achieving. Plenty on reading, writing, math, problem-solving, creative thinking. Everything for parents who want to help but not push their children.

226 pages, 6 x 9, illustrations,
Quality paperback, $10.95

THE BROWN BAG COOKBOOK
Nutritious Portable Lunches for Kids and Grown-Ups
by Sara Sloan

Now in its ninth printing this popular book has more than 1,000 brown bag lunch ideas with 150 recipes for simple, quick, nutritious lunches that kids will love. Breakfast ideas, too! The more people care what they eat, the more popular this book becomes.

192 pages, 8¼ x 7¼, illustrations,
Quality paperback, $9.95

Easy-to-Make TEDDY BEARS AND ALL THE TRIMMINGS
by Jodie Davis

Now you can make the most lovable, huggable, plain or fancy teddy bears imaginable, for a fraction of store-bought costs. Step-by-step instructions and easy patterns drawn to actual size for large, soft-bodied bears, quilted bears, and even jointed bears. Plus patterns for clothes, accessories—even teddy bear furniture!

192 pages, 8½ x 11, illustrations and patterns,
Quality paperback, $13.95

To Order: At your bookstore or order directly from Williamson Publishing. We accept Visa and MasterCard (please include number and expiration date), or send check to:

Williamson Publishing Company
Church Hill Road, P.O. Box 185
Charlotte, Vermont 05445

Toll-free phone orders with credit cards: 1-800-234-8791

Please add $2.00 for postage and handling. Satisfaction is guaranteed or full refund without questions or quibbles.